1968

University of St. Francis
GEN   827.52 H948
Hunting
Jonathan Swift

3 0301 00033150 0

W9-ABR-666

Twayne's English Authors Series

Robert Hunting

PURDUE UNIVERSITY

Jonathan Swift

 42

TEVE AI

Jonathan Swift

By ROBERT HUNTING

Purdue University

Twayne Publishers, Inc. :: New York

LIBRARY
College of St. Francis
JOLIET, ILL.

Copyright © 1967 by Twayne Publishers, Inc.

All Rights Reserved

Library of Congress Catalog Card Number: 66–28909

MANUFACTURED IN THE UNITED STATES OF AMERICA

827.52
H948

23.26

43486

FOR C. S. AND M.

Preface

This study of Jonathan Swift (1667–1745) is intended to interest people who want an introduction to his best prose and poetry. It will no doubt be but one of the numerous publications that will mark the three-hundredth anniversary (1667–1967) of Swift's birth.

In assembling the materials of this book I have relied very heavily on an impressive body of historical criticism, but my approach has been only incidentally that of the historical critic. Rather, my aim has been, in the first place, to view in loosely chronological order those of Swift's writings which promise almost certainly to be eternally contemporaneous and which, therefore, speak most interestingly and often very insistently to our times. My aim has been, in the second place, to attempt to indicate as little as possible the right and the wrong way to read these works and, as much as possible, to indicate what might be termed an area of interpretation, in and for our time, that a thoughtful reading invites.

These principles of selection and criticism obligate me to avoid —or, at least, to touch only lightly upon—a large number of alluring historical, bibliographical, and biographical questions and a number of writings (like the *History of the Four Last Years of the Queen*) that reward study but are so closely tied to their times that they are outside the scope of this book. (However, one convenient but unplanned result of these limitations is that the study of the writings which this book focuses on may be made to constitute just about a semester's work in a course or a seminar on Swift.) The plan of this book also forces me to make no more than passing comment about the literary influences at work on Swift and about Swift's influence on literary figures who follow him. However, by consulting the bibliography a reader will discover that the very rich resources of Swift criticism and scholarship will lead him through any of these, and many other, profitable areas of inquiry.

Every writer must envy the assurance with which Montaigne was able to deceive himself in his *Essays:* "Reader, this is an honest book." I have tried to make my book honest; I hope it is. At least in matters where honesty is relatively easy, I should most especially like not to err. Therefore, wherever in the following pages an interpretation of a fact or a pattern of facts is my own, I have tried to indicate this as diffidently as possible to my readers. In the very many places where I have accepted useful discoveries or insights of the great Swift scholars and critics of our and earlier times, I have tried always to indicate that fact. My indebtedness to these men is as obvious as it is enormous; for, in common with all Swift students, I have perforce relied heavily on the absolutely indispensable contributions to Swift criticism and scholarship made by such men as Émile Pons, F. Elrington Ball, Harold Williams, Ricardo Quintana, Herbert Davis, Louis Landa, and Irvin Ehrenpreis. I am also indebted, though in a different way, to the ideas of my students who have courageously supported minority positions in term papers or class discussions about Swift. I owe much, in addition, to Constance Coulter Hunting.

My hope is, finally, that readers will say that the seven chapters between these covers are, to use a favorite circumlocution of one of my favorite friends, "not entirely without merit." If the circumlocution is at all applicable, then this book may encourage an interest in both Swift the man and Swift the writer. That would be good, for then some readers would go on to read better and in all senses bigger books than mine could ever be about this most interesting, disturbing, and perplexing of the Augustans.

Swift's EPITAPH, which I quote in Chapter 1, is from *Collected Poems,* by W. B. Yeats, copyright 1933 by The Macmillan Company, used by permission of The Macmillan Company, Mrs. W. B. Yeats, and The Macmillan Company of Canada, Ltd.

ROBERT HUNTING

Purdue University

Contents

Chronology

1660– Reign of Charles II.
1685
1680– Approximate terminal dates of the English Augustan Age.
1740 F. R. Leavis, in a helpful capsule description of this age,
writes, ". . . a metropolitan fashionable Society, compact
and politically in the ascendant, found itself in charge
of standards, and extremely convinced that, in the things
it cared about, there were standards to be observed, models
to be followed: it was anxious to be civilized on the best
models." (*Revaluations*, 112–13). Chief literary figures:
Dryden, Congreve, Addison, Steele, Swift, Gay, Defoe, and
Pope.

1667 Jonathan Swift born in Dublin, Ireland, November 30, to
Abigaile and, posthumously, to Jonathan Swift.

1673(?)– Attended Kilkenny Grammar School
1681

1678 Popish Plot.

1679 Origin of the Whig and Tory parties.

1682– Swift at Trinity College, Dublin. Graduated *speciali gratia*,
1686 along with four others in his class of thirty-eight students.

1685– Reign of James II.
1688

1688 The Glorious Revolution and the beginning of the reign
of William and Mary (1688–1702). Trouble in Ireland.
Trinity College closed. Swift went to England.

1689 He became secretary in the household of Sir William Temple, Moor Park, Surrey, England. Here he probably first
met Esther Johnson ("Stella"), whom he tutored during
the years with Temple.

1690 Swift returned to Ireland. Battle of the Boyne, in eastern
Ireland, in which William III defeated James II.

1691 Swift rejoined the Temple household.

1692 M. A., Oxford. First published poem: "Ode to the Athenian Society."

1695 Ordained as priest in the Church of Ireland (the Irish branch of the Anglican Church). Made Vicar of Kilroot in northern Ireland.

1696 Returned to Moor Park. While with Sir William Temple, 1696–1699, Swift probably composed most of *A Tale of a Tub.*

1699 Death of Temple. Swift returned to Ireland, as chaplain to Lord Berkeley.

1700 Presented parish of Laracor, Ireland, and prebend at St. Patrick's Cathedral, Dublin.

1700 or 1701 Esther Johnson and Rebecca Dingley settled in Dublin.

1701 Awarded D. D., from Dublin University.

1702– Reign of Queen Anne.
1714

1704 Battle of Blenheim. Great victory for Marlborough and the English. *A Tale of a Tub, The Battle of the Books,* and *The Mechanical Operation of the Spirit* published anonymously. Also (*ca.* 1704), *A Meditation upon a Broomstick.*

1707 Swift in London, emissary of the Irish clergy, seeking remission of "first fruits" (a tax on Irish clerical incomes).

1708 *The Partridge-Bickerstaff Papers.*

1709 Back at Laracor, in Ireland. "A Description of the Morning."

1710 Tories come to power. Swift returned to England. "A Description of a City Shower." Renounced Whigs to join Tories. Editor of *The Examiner,* the Tory newspaper; *The Journal to Stella* (continued from September 1, 1710 to June 6, 1713).

1711 *Argument Against Abolishing Christianity; The Conduct of the Allies; Miscellanies in Prose and Verse; A New Journey to Paris.*

1713 Treaty of Utrecht, ending the War of the Spanish Succession. Swift appointed Dean of St. Patrick's Cathedral, Dublin. "Cadenus and Vanessa" written (later revised; published 1727).

1714 Formation of the Scriblerus Club. "The Author Upon Himself." Reign of George I begins (1714–1727). Beginning of long Whig supremacy under Walpole.

1716 Presumed by some biographers to have married Stella.

1720 *A Proposal for the Universal Use of Irish Manufacture;* probable beginning of composition of *Gulliver's Travels.*

1721 *A Letter to a Young Gentleman, lately entered into Holy Orders.*

1722 "Satirical Elegy on the Death of a late Famous General" [Marlborough].

1723 *A Letter to a Young Lady on her Marriage.*

1724– *The Drapier Letters.*
1725

1726 Visit to England, where he was Alexander Pope's house-guest; *Gulliver's Travels* published.

1727 Last trip to England. Pope-Swift *Miscellanies,* vols. I and II published ("Cadenus and Vanessa" included in this publication). Reign of George II begins (1727–1760).

1728 Death of Stella. Pope-Swift *Miscellanies,* vol. III.

1729 "A Pastoral Dialogue"; *A Modest Proposal.*

1731 "A Beautiful Young Nymph Going to Bed"; "Verses on the Death of Dr. Swift."

1732 Pope-Swift *Miscellanies,* vol. IV (self-styled "third"); "A Lady's Dressing Room."

1735 Collected edition of Swift's *Works,* published in Dublin, by George Faulkner.

1736 Pope-Swift *Miscellanies,* vol. V; "A Character, Panegyric, and Description of the Legion Club."

1737 *A Proposal for Giving Badges to the Beggars in all the Parishes of Dublin.*

1738 *A Compleat Collection of genteel and ingenious Conversation.*

1742 Guardians in Chancery appointed to care for Swift's affairs.

1745 Swift died, October 19.

CHAPTER 1

Life and Literature for Our Times

JOHN PARTRIDGE was a cobbler who became a highly successful maker of almanacs. Three times—in 1699, 1704, and in 1706—he challenged his readers to compete with him at prophecy. In 1708 Jonathan Swift took up the challenge, not only I suppose for the fun he could have in attacking so arrant a hypocrite, and not only because he very commonly felt a need to unmask fakery, but also because Partridge had attacked the clergy of the Church of England;[1] and Swift was a clergyman, and the Church of England was his church. Swift's astonishing procedure is a good introduction to this unusual man of the eighteenth century. First, in the invented role of Isaac Bickerstaff, he prophesied the death of Partridge. It was, he said, "but a trifle; yet I will mention it, . . . [Partridge] will infallibly die upon the 29th of March next, about eleven at Night, of a raging fever."[2] Later, adopting another pose, he reported "the accomplishment of the first of Mr. Bickerstaff's predictions": Partridge was dead. "Mr. Bickerstaff was mistaken almost four Hours in his Calculation. In other Circumstances he was exact enough."[3] Swift did not, even at this point let up; he also celebrated his victim's "death" with an elegy:

> Here Five Foot deep lyes on his Back
> A Cobler, Starmonger, and Quack,
> Who to the Stars in pure Good-will,
> Does to his best look upward still. (1708)

So convincing was Swift's merciless hazing that the Stationer's Register removed Partridge's name from the rolls. Poor Partridge himself, however, remained quite stubbornly unconvinced and in his 1709 almanac vigorously protested that he was alive; but Swift would have none of this. In *A Vindication of Isaac Bickerstaff, Esq.*, he conclusively proved the death and ridiculed Partridge for not having the sense to admit it: "He is the *only* person," wrote the satirist, "from whom I have heard . . . Objection. . . ." [4]

Jonathan Swift, the perpetrator of this weird and hugely successful hoax, was to spend a large part of his life defending his church from attackers. All his long life he invented masks—Bickerstaff, Drapier, Gulliver—which fooled nobody for long; but through them he effectively made known his ideas and attitudes. All his life he attacked pretense and pleaded with people to see that "It is not as you think—look!" [5] His hope was that, if people looked, they would see behind the successful almanac-maker, the charlatan; beneath the rind, the kernel; behind the appearance, the reality. That Swift sometimes ignored or even perverted his own teaching does not detract from his preachment. No one, ever, has said more powerfully what this man had to say.

I *Swift's Background*

Jonathan Swift was born on November 30, 1667, in Hoey's Alley, in Dublin. Born after the death of his father, he was the second child and first son of English parents who had moved to Ireland. Thus far most, if not all, biographers agree. Almost immediately, however, fiction has usually taken over. A great number of fictional lives of Swift have, in fact, been written. The point may be illustrated by reference to one of the most delightful of them. It is by Elbert Hubbard (1856–1915) who, in his *Little Journeys to the Homes of the Great*, wrote,

His father married at twenty. His income matched his years—it was just twenty pounds per annum. His wife was a young girl, bright, animated, intelligent.

In a few short months this girl carried in her arms a baby [Jane, Swift's sister]. This baby was wrapped in a tattered shawl and cried piteously from hunger, for the mother had not enough to eat. She was cold, and sick, and in disgrace. Her husband, too, was ill, and sorely in debt. It was midwinter.

When Spring came, and the flowers blossomed, and the birds mated, and warm breezes came whispering softly from the South, and all the earth was glad, the husband of this child-wife was in his grave, and she was alone. Alone? No; she carried in her arms the hungry babe, and beneath her heart she felt the faint flutter of another life.[6]

That "faint flutter" was Jonathan Swift.

An equally astonishing account may be found in Phyllis Greenacre's *Swift and Carroll, A Psychoanalytic Study of Two Lives.* Among other interesting theses, Dr. Greenacre suggests that "Swift apparently suffered from severe anxiety and diffuse hypochondriasis of the type which so often accompanies an unusually severe castration complex, in which pregenital determinants are strong." [7] Dr. Greenacre also says that "Swift's early life would certainly predispose to the development of a stunting bisexuality, as indeed his mature years showed. That there was further fixation at the anal level and an extreme impairment of genital functioning is indicated in his character and his writings." [8] I do not find such speculations very convincing, especially in this instance, because of insufficient and even inexact use of supporting evidence. For example, the use of the *Memoirs of Scriblerus* as evidence about Jonathan Swift is most distressing since there were six other writers involved in the composition of that book; moreover, the authorship of the various contributions has never been settled.

More responsible scholarship, particularly that of the past few decades, has been increasingly successful in disentangling fact from fiction in the life of Swift. To the results of this research—specifically to the biographical chapters of such books as *Swift, the Man, his Works, and the Age,* by Irvin Ehrenpreis—the brief, following biographical account is heavily indebted.

Reared in Dublin by his relatives, Swift attended Kilkenny Grammar School and, later, Trinity College, Dublin. He could not have received, in Ireland, a better education; but he appears to have been no more than a run-of-the-mill student. At Dublin he insulted a junior dean and was obliged publicly, on bended knee, to beg the dean's pardon; [9] and, though he did well in language and literature, he did poorly in what he disliked: abstract philosophy and formal rhetoric.[10] He did receive his degree "by special grace," as every biographer says; but "this favour," Professor Ehrenpreis shows, "was by no means uncommon." In Swift's class

of thirty-eight students, five graduated *"speciali gratia."* [11] Thus
Swift was himself quite misleading when he wrote in the fragment of an autobiography which he prepared in 1714:
". . . when the time came for taking his degree of Batchlor, . . .
he was stopped of his Degree, for Dullness and Insufficiency, and
at last hardly admitted in a manner little to his Credit, which is
called in that Colle[d]ge *Specialia* gratia. . . ." [12]

During most of the decade ending in 1699, Swift was secretary
to a retired statesman, Sir William Temple, at Moor Park, Surrey,
in England. Sir William Temple (1628–99), one of the great statesmen of the seventeenth century, is remembered for his work in or-
ganizing the triple alliance (England, Holland, Sweden) and for
arranging the marriage of William of Orange and Mary. Esther
Johnson ("Stella") and, later, Swift were inhabitants of his home
during his years of retirement at Moor Park. On his behalf, as we
shall see, Swift engaged himself in the war between the Ancients
and the Moderns in *The Battle of the Books.* After his death,
Swift edited his *Letters* (1701). Swift's stay with this great man
was interrupted several times, most notably from May, 1694, to
May, 1696, when Swift was ordained and went as rector to Kilroot
parish in the north of Ireland.

But the years with Temple were important not only in that
turbulent age because of the urbane and civilizing influence of
the Temple household, but also because they were years when
Swift could (and did) read widely in the Temple library; because he had opportunity to find what he was, and was not, as a
poet; because he discovered his gifts as a satirist—most of *A Tale
of a Tub* was written during these years (though not published
until 1704); and because he there met Esther Johnson. He is presumed by many biographers to have married Esther Johnson
("Stella") in 1716. The question of whether he did or did not is
a much debated one, and the fairest statement to make is simply that the evidence is inconclusive.[13] Evidence does say that
shortly after Temple's death, Esther Johnson and her friend Rebecca Dingley (she was older than Stella) settled permanently in
Dublin, near Swift.

Harold Williams states that Swift and Stella "observed an almost
exaggerated propriety. Whether at Dublin or Laracor, the ladies
were free of his lodgings, or house, only when Swift was away. In

Dublin, upon his return, they removed elsewhere; or, when he was in the country, they found rooms in Trim, occupied a little cottage at Laracor, or were the guests of Dr. Raymond. Further, Swift hardly allowed himself at any time to be left alone in the same room with Stella." [14] In these almost unbelievable terms, this relationship continued for more than a quarter of a century. The facts of the relationship, where indeed they are facts, and if indeed they are facts, so cry out for interpretation and resolution that it is no wonder that much has been written on the subject. I have no new evidence to offer and therefore must leave the problem unresolved. It does *seem* to me that no marriage took place.

During the Moor Park years Swift also experienced the first of those terrible attacks which—as with Dostoevsky and his epilepsy—were to dominate all his years. Swift describes his illness thus in his autobiographical fragment: "For he [Swift] happened before twenty years old, by a Surfeit of fruit to contract a giddyness and coldness of Stomach, that almost brought him to his Grave, and this disorder pursued him with Intermissions of two or three years to the end of his Life." [15] The "surfeit of fruit" is unlikely to have been the cause of a lifelong misery. Opinion is now general that the suffering was caused by Ménière's Disease, a disturbance of the inner ear, the symptoms of which are giddiness and vertigo. The disease had then, and has now, no known cure. However, people who suffer from it are told today to take the pills that are more commonly prescribed against seasickness. "And then," Irvin Ehrenpreis reports, "they usually have no trouble." [16] In an era that knew nothing of this simple palliative, Swift suffered his "trouble" through all his adult life.

II 1708–1714

The years 1708 to 1714 were among the most exciting in Swift's lengthy career. He was in London much of this time, having been sent there as a petitioner for the Irish Church. He became involved first with the Whigs and then, since he was a man of an innately conservative bent, with the Tories. (Also, the Tories were disposed to grant his petition.) These were the years of *The Bickerstaff Papers;* of two fine poems, "the Description of the Morning," and "A Description of a City Shower"; of the editorship of the Tory journal, *The Examiner;* of that brilliant piece of Tory pamphleteering, *The Conduct of the Allies;* of *The Journal to Stella;* and so on. These were also the days of close association with the chief ministers of England, Harley and Bolingbroke. As Swift wrote in his *Four Last Years,* ". . . it was my lot to have been daily conversant with the persons then in power; never absent in times of business or conversation, until a few weeks before her Majesty's death; and a witness of almost every step they made in the course of their administration. . . ." [17] Therefore, when he writes about princes, about politics, about government—as he does in *A Tale of a Tub,* in *Gulliver's Travels,* and in many of his poems and essays—he does so with the authority of considerable experience.

These were also the days of close and happy friendship with many of the chief wits and writers of the day: Parnell, Pope, Bolingbroke, Prior, Arbuthnot, and Gay. With some of these he formed the Scriblerus Club, a group which planned, among other projects, a burlesque report of a voyage. This project is probably the origin of *Gulliver's Travels.* And these were years, finally, of professional disappointment. In a generation when a worldly church lived contentedly with the concept that churchly offices were political spoil,[18] Swift, who had so brilliantly served his party, had good reason to expect the reward of a deanery or a bishopric in England. Instead, in 1713, he was given a deanery in Dublin, and for a reason that is not clear. Swift himself blamed the Duchess of Somerset and John Sharp, the Archibishop of York, who, he believed, had unfavorably called Queen Anne's attention to *A Tale of a Tub.* Other factors were no doubt involved. At any rate, it was back to Ireland that Swift went, in 1714, to "die," he later reported, "like a poisoned rat in a hole." [19] He was forty-seven years old. To Stella he wrote, ". . . neither can I feel Joy at passing my days in Irel[an]d, . . . and I confess I thought the Ministry would not let me go; but perhaps th[e]y cant help it." [20]

III   *1714–1745*

The thirty-one years from 1714 to 1745 were the Irish years that began with a period of some considerable hurt and disappointment. However, always the conscientious clergyman, Swift busied himself with deanery chores. And, though during the first few years he wrote little, he did exercise regularly, even when the weather was bad; there were always the deanery stairs which he could walk up and down, up and down, and up and down again.[21] Personal cleanliness being always important to him, he no doubt continued to wash himself "with," as Samuel Johnson caustically wrote in his *Life of Swift*, "oriental scrupulosity." His circle of friends was gradually enlarged, and included such people as Archbishop William King, John Ford, Daniel Jackson, Knightley Chetwode, Patrick Delany, Thomas Sheridan, the Rochforts, and the Grattans, in addition to Esther Johnson and Rebeccah Dingley. Enigmatically on the edge of things, but always very much there, was also Esther Vanhomrigh. Miss Vanhomrigh—the "Vanessa" of Swift's poem, "Cadenus and Vanessa"—is the unhappy lady who fell in love with Swift during his London years and who followed him to Ireland, where she died in 1723.

In a poem entitled "To Charles Ford Esq. on his Birth-day" (1723), Swift wrote,

> I thought my very Spleen would burst
> When Fortune hither [to Ireland] drove me first;
> Was full as hard to please as You,
> Nor Persons Names, nor Places knew;
> But now I act as other Folk,
> Like Pris'ners when their Gall is broke.

The words reveal that Swift had slowly reconciled himself to his life in Ireland. Indeed, life was far from over for him; in fact, the 1720's usher in a period of almost unbelievable creativity, including his writing of *The Drapier Letters* (1724–25)—letters that made him a national hero in Ireland; *Gulliver's Travels* (1726); *A Modest Proposal* (1729); and much of his best poetry, like a "Satirical Elegy on the Death of a late Famous General" (1722), "A Beautiful Young Nymph Going to Bed" (1721), and "On Poetry: A Rapsody" (1733).

Swift, the great "Irish Patriot" occasionally gives the impression that Irish affairs did not interest him. His own very considerable activities in behalf of the Irish belie this impression.[22] His *Drapier Letters* saved Ireland from Wood's halfpence,[23] in 1724–25. Earlier, and in fact breaking the long silence after Swift's 1714 retreat from England, had come A *Proposal For the Universal Use of Irish Manufacture* (1720). A little later, in 1729, were published both his A *Proposal That all the Ladies and Women of Ireland should appear constantly in Irish Manufactures* and A *Modest Proposal.* We shall learn, too, that his poetry and correspondence confirm an irritated but abiding fascination with Irish affairs.

However, the temptation is to make of this "Hibernian patriot" a different kind of patriot than he really was. Swift was no fiery revolutionary. In his *Of Publick Absurdityes* in England he wrote: "I am grossly deceived if any sober man of very moderate talents, when he reflects upon the many ridiculous hurtfull maxims, customs, and generall rules of life which prevail in this kingdom, would not with great reason be tempted, according to the present turn of his humor, either to laugh, lament, or be angry, or if he were sanguin enough, perhaps to dream of a remedy. It is the mistake of wise and good men that they expect more Reason and Virtue from human nature, than taking it in the bulk, it is in any sort capable of." [24] The attitude reflected in this characteristically pessimistic and conservative comment is perhaps the sort of thing that impelled George Orwell to his revealing remark: "[Swift's] implied aim [in his writings] is a static, incurious civilization—the world of his way day, a little cleaner, a little saner, with no radical change and no poking into the unknowable." [25]

When Swift speaks in behalf of the Irish, we should not expect to hear notes quite out of his range. In fairness we should be more reasonable in our expectations than was Orwell, for what Orwell wanted to hear were notes out of most people's range in those years. Orwell would have been more pleased with another long-time Irish resident and contemporary of Swift, William Penn (1644–1718), who was in many ways a bigger man than Swift and whose political and religious pronouncements with respect to Pennsylvania show him to be well ahead of his times. The significant differences between these men are that Swift could write quite a lot better, and in theological and political matters Swift was very much more of his period than was Penn. This means that Swift could not be, and certainly was not, a front-line patriot arguing, as Orwell would have liked (and as Orwell would have done), for the rights of all the people of a distressed island. In truth, the ironic fact is that this Irish patriot of the eighteenth century was a spokesman of but one segment of the English people resident in Ireland. "What [Swift] overlooked is, to be sure, amazing to us today," writes Ricardo Quintana; "for the native Irish were wholly excluded from his community of free men, and of the Anglo-Irish only those conforming to the Established Church [Swift's church] had full rights." [26]

IV Old Age

Swift's last years are sometimes introduced by a reference to the story told by Edward Young. Looking at a dying elm tree, Swift is said to have declared, "I shall be like that tree, I shall die at the top." [27] The account of these final years commonly goes on to mention Samuel Johnson's remarkable declaration in "The Vanity of Human Wishes": "Swift expires a driv'ler and a show." Edward Young's report may safely be accepted; but Johnson's great line simply is not true. Professor Ehrenpreis remarks that "Swift was no more neurotic than Pope or Johnson, and probably less so. The tradition of his madness has been rejected for forty years by every qualified scholar who has bothered to look into the question." [28]

The facts of Swift's last years are for the most part the not unfamiliar facts about a man who grew old. On into the 1730's—Swift was then in his middle and late sixties—he worked at his job, presiding over chapter meetings at the deanery, listening carefully and critically to the sermons of young preachers in his cathedral, and performing his extensive charities.[29] Hawkesworth, referring to the years after 1724, writes that "Over the populace [Swift] was the most absolute monarch that ever governed men, and he was regarded by persons of every rank with veneration and esteem." [30] Such facts make fiction of the generally held beliefs about Swift's old age. In his seventieth year he wrote to Pope that, walking through the streets of Dublin, he received "a thousand hats and blessings." [31] Those are not the words of, and that is not the reception given to, "a driv'ler and a show."

But Swift increasingly in the late 1730's withdrew from society. In addition to the vertigo and deafness associated with Ménière's Disease, he began to suffer more and more from bad memory and poor eyesight. Clearly incapable of carrying on his normal duties, he appointed in 1739 a subdean to preside over meet-

LIBRARY
College of St. Francis
JOLIET, ILL.

43486

ings of the cathedral chapter.[32] In 1742 (aged seventy-five), Swift was put under the care of a committee of guardians—not because he was mad, but because, as Ehrenpreis points out, "it was the most convenient way for a senile person, living alone, to be defended against various sorts of exploitation.[33]

The remaining years of his life are very sad ones. He spoke little, and when told on his birthday in 1743 that Dubliners were going to celebrate the event with bonfires and illuminations, he said, "It is all folly, they had better let it alone." [34] In 1745 he died and was buried, near Stella, in St. Patrick's Cathedral, beneath the famous Latin epitaph which he himself had composed: *"Hic depositum est Corpus/* Jonathan Swift, . . . *ubi saeva Indignatio/ Ulterious/ Cor lacerare nequit/ Abi Viator/ Et imitare, si poteris,/ Strenuum pro virili/ Libertatis Vindicatorem."* Yeats's version of this famous epitaph is:

> Swift sailed into his rest;
> Savage indignation there
> Cannot lacerate his breast.
> Imitate him if you dare,
> World-besotted traveller; he
> Served human liberty.

In his own way, Swift did serve human liberty. However, this ideal of service—combined with his lifelong alertness against any form of pomposity and sentimentality, and his sardonic vision of reality—seems less well expressed by his epitaph than by the major legacy in his will: he left money to establish, "in or near Dublin," a hospital for "ideots and lunaticks," because, as he said in one of his poems, "No Nation wanted [i.e., *needed*] it so much." [35]

V *The Best of Jonathan Swift, the Writer*

Jonathan Swift was a writer for almost half a century. His first published poem was the "Ode to the Athenian Society" (1691); his last poem of consequence was "A Character, Panegyric, and Description of the Legion Club" (1736). The words in prose bridge almost as many decades, for, as he tells us in the "Apology" to his *A Tale of a Tub,* "the great part" of that book was finished in 1696; the long trail initiated in 1696, and perhaps even earlier, ended in 1738 with the publication of the "Compleat Collection of genteel and ingenious Conversation." During these nearly fifty years, Swift wrote a great deal—in fact, an almost unbelievable amount when we remember that writing was not his main preoccupation. Herbert Davis' great Shakespeare Head edition of *The Prose Works of Jonathan Swift* includes thirteen volumes (minus the index); Harold Williams' edition of the poetry of Swift embraces three volumes; and another two volumes make up the Williams edition of Swift's *Journal to Stella...*

Looking at this extensive body of writing, Herbert Reed comments: "All that Swift wrote is empirical, experiencial, *actuel* [his italics]. It is impossible to detach it from circumstances; we must consider each book or pamphlet in relation to its political intention." [36] With the first part of this quotation we can agree immediately because anything that anybody writes is inevitably in one sense or another "empirical, experiencial, *actuel.*" With the second part of the quotation I have trouble, however; for, in the first place, Swift wrote a number of things that quite clearly have little or no "political intention." We think at once of the many poems to Stella, for example; of the pamphlet entitled *A Proposal for Correcting, Improving and Ascertaining the English Tongue* (1712); of the *Letter to a Young Gentleman, lately entered into Holy Orders* (1720); or of the *Letter to a Young Lady on her Marriage* (1723). Of much greater concern to me, however, is an assertion that "It is impossible to detach [any work by Swift] from circumstances. . . ." Mr. Reed does qualify his position somewhat with the remark that, "though none of Swift's works can be separated from its historical occasion, historical considerations cannot usurp aesthetic judgement." [37] However, my inclination would be to rephrase the sentence and allow it to say this: "Of course aesthetic judgment must not be usurped; moreover the emphatic testimony of the centuries is that such judgments are very generally made without much regard for historical considerations." Therefore, for almost three hundred years Swift's readers have been quietly separating Swift's works from the circumstances that produced them. In fact, if the work may not be separated, it is not much read. This has been the fate, for example, of *The Drapier Letters* (1724–25). Very little of what is usually called "background" knowledge is needed to make these *Letters* (especially the fourth one) vastly entertaining and instructive. But at least some special knowledge is needed, and the result is that for each reader of *The Drapier Letters* there are, I would suppose, several thousand readers of *Gulliver's Travels* (1726), a book which can be and usually is separated from its "historic occasion."

The neglect of *The Drapier Letters* is to be lamented. However, it is apparently one of the laws of literary survival: the book that cannot be "detached" from the "historic occasion" becomes a kind of dead monument, monumentally ignored. To survive, any form of art—a play, a novel, or a prose satire—must transcend its occasion and speak forcefully and eloquently to those who know little or nothing about the occasion. Some scholars regret that a reader's ignorance causes him to give to a piece of literature a different reading from that intended by the author, or a reading that is even inappropriate to the circumstances that produced it. However, since the passage of years makes such different or "wrong" readings inevitable, and since these different or "wrong" readings always offer at least the theoretical possibility of being an improvement on the reading originally intended and/or given, I suggest that we may view these changes stoically and that, though we may sometimes sigh, we should never sob about this matter. Indeed, for me the only real regret is that occasionally something very good, like *The Drapier Letters,* suffers—because of this law—the fate of not getting much attention except from specialists.

The works which I analyze and assess in the following chapters have transcended the occasion which produced them. In that sense, they are "the best of Swift." To know something of the background of these great works is very often a tremendously revealing and enriching experience; and our attention to such background information is justified and essential to the extent that it reveals and enriches the document we are studying. The danger is that the searching out and the analysis of this background information may become, in itself, so major a concern that the document is either forgotten or unconsciously or even deliberately overlooked by critics who do not see the need for, or would actually be embarrassed by, any attempt to judge a piece of writing. This danger I have tried to avoid by keeping the document (the poem, the essay, the prose satire) always at the center of attention. And I have, along with my analyses, made many judgments; for it seems to me that analysis and assessment are the very best bedfellows. As I have said, the scope of my discussion has been severely limited to those magical creations, "the best of Swift," which have transcended the circumstances that gave them birth.

CHAPTER 2

"For the Universal Improvement of Mankind"

I   An Overview of the Tale-volume

SWIFT'S first great prose work was *A Tale of a Tub*. It was published in 1704, though written about a half a dozen years earlier, in a volume which also contained *The Battle of the Books* and *The Mechanical Operation of the Spirit*. Like most of his work, it was issued anonymously and earned Swift no money; and also like most of his work, it was, as the charming candor of the subtitle informs us, "Written for the Universal Improvement of Mankind." Part of the volume—most specifically *The Battle of the Books*—was originally written to aid his patron, Sir William Temple, in a controversy between the "Ancients" and the "Moderns." [1]

In his *Essay upon the Ancient and Modern Learning* (1692), Temple had upheld the superiority of the Ancients. He attempted to refute what seemed to him to be the two essential points of the Moderns: the first was that Nature, always constant, must produce genius as great today as yesterday or tomorrow; the second was that the Moderns, profiting from the great store of riches in their heritage, must necessarily surpass the Ancients. Émile Pons summarizes Temple's conclusion accurately and succinctly: "Our age has none of the greatness of ancient times. Even in the experimental sciences, where we think we are superior, we do not really compare. 'Has Harvey outdone Hippocrates, or Wilkins, Archimedes?'" Pons then comments as follows: "Temple's complete incomprehension of the scientific discoveries of his day is characteristic and aids us in better understanding Swift's indifference. His admiration for the literature of the Ancients blocks his horizon. It prevents him not only from understanding his own times but also from differentiating what is truly admirable in antiquity from what is not. His admiration is thoroughly conventional and, because it is interwoven with error and superstition, he makes the famous mistake which was to bring him so much badgering." [2]

Temple's serious blunder occurred in his comment that "The two most ancient [books] that I know of in prose among those we call profane authors, are Aesop's Fables and Phalaris's Epistles, both living near the same time, which was that of Cyrus and Pythagoras." This error was not challenged by clever young William Wotton, the first of the Moderns to reply to Temple. However, Temple's error was dramatically and emphatically revealed in 1697 when Wotton issued a second edition of his *Reflections upon Ancient and Modern Learning*, which included Richard Bentley's *Dissertation on the Epistles of Phalaris*. Bentley, a great scholar, said, and proved, that the *Epistles of Phalaris* and the *Fables* were spurious. For example, Phalaris could not have written the epistles with which he was credited: they mention cities that were not in existence during the life of Phalaris. Such a disclosure was a victory for the Moderns. However, Richard Bentley had personally offended Charles Boyle when, as a student at Oxford, Boyle was asked to edit the *Epistles*. One essential manuscript necessary for him to complete his assignment was in St. James's Library, the king's library where Bentley was keeper. Bentley did not seem to Boyle to be sufficiently helpful; therefore Boyle, later the Earl of Orrery, was moved to comment publicly and ironically on "the singular humanity" (meaning, of course, "inhumanity") of Richard Bentley. Obviously Modern Learning was ill-mannered and needed chastisement; and this disclosure was a victory for the Ancients.

The quarrel seems obviously to have bogged down on occasion into irrelevancies. Indeed, we should not be surprised that even Swift was apparently not much concerned about the central philosophical issues. We recall that, in college, "he did poorly in what he would always dislike—abstract philosophy and formal rhetoric." [3] However, it is clear enough that what initially impelled him into the fray was the perfectly reasonable desire to support his patron and friend, Sir William Temple.

A Tale of a Tub was published in 1704; but, as mentioned above, it was written earlier. How much earlier and what was written when are interesting questions that can only in part be answered. Some dates may be mentioned with confidence: for example, the "Epistle Dedicatory" is subscribed 1697; the "Conclusion" has a reference to the *Histoire de M. Constance*, which Swift read in 1697,[4] so we may date the "Conclusion" as very probably written in that year. Perhaps he had sketched out the kernel of his story, or had written some parts of it—maybe the religious allegory—when he was a student at Trinity College.[5] Swift himself does not help us much with this problem, except that he does say, in the "Apology" inserted in the 1710 edition of the *Tale*, that "The greatest part of that book was finished above thirteen years since, 1696, which is eight years before it was published."

In any case, the dates are not of crucial importance to this study. More pertinent is the subject matter of the *Tale*, and fortunately on this point we are given help by the author. He announces his subject as "abuses in Religion" and in "learning." Thus, if we accept his near enough guess about the date (1696) as the year when he finished "the greatest part" of the *Tale*, then we may not unreasonably assume that he put aside this work in 1697 to help Temple by writing *The Battle of the Books* as a satire on the Moderns—especially on the false learning of the Moderns. This task completed, but the work for some reason remaining in manuscript form[6]—it may have been that Temple, who was not overly fond of satire, advised against publication—Swift returned to his *Tale* and its religious allegory.

At this point, perhaps seeing that corruptions in learning (the subject of the *Battle*) and in religion (the subject of the *Tale*) have a common denominator[7]—irrationality being the cause of both—he put his two books between one set of covers. He then dove-tailed his *Battle* to the *Tale* by the use of the so-called digressions (actually thematic tenons from the *Battle*) which attacked false learning—"A Digressions Concerning Critics," "A Digression in the Modern Kind," etc.,—and added the section entitled *The Mechanical Operation of the Spirit*.

Such a series of conjectures is consistent with the comment in the "Apology" to the *Tale*, where Swift declares exactly his plan: "the abuses in Religion, he proposed to set forth in the Allegory of the Coats, and the three Brothers, which was to make up the body of the discourse. Those in learning he chose to introduce by way of digressions." Swift also may have sensed that the narrator who pretended to be the author of the *Battle,* of the digressions, and of *The Mechanical Operation of the Spirit* was a type fortunately not inconsistent with the narrator who pretended to be the author of the *Tale.* So, with a single basic theme and with a single narrator to give some semblance of consistency to the tone and point of view, he was enabled to make one book of the various parts he had started with. (This book I shall hereinafter refer to as the *Tale*-volume.) But these conjectures must be most cautiously advanced since they cannot in any sense be proved. We must allow, however, that the ironic comment in Section V of the *Tale* reads very much like a confesson of his own method: ". . . I have known some authors [who] enclose digressions in one another, like a nest of boxes." The "nest of boxes" is an apt description for the book which he bequeathed to us in the 1704 and again in the edition of 1710.

A work accomplished in the way that Swift accomplished the *Tale*-volume is almost inevitably lacking in unity and cohesion. That the book succeeds as well as it does, and that it can be read as a book with a beginning, a middle, and an end, is explained somewhat fancifully, but I think not unreasonably, by Pons's supposition that Swift turned to his manuscript—adding to it and editing it—only when he found his inspiration and his temperament tuned to a certain, and generally the same, key.[8] The book would have achieved much greater unity if, to shift the metaphor, Swift had been more expert at the mortise and tenon work necessary to make one book out of many. He was not expert at this art: we witness the familiar inconsistencies not only in the *Tale*-volume but also in *Gulliver's Travels.*[9] Furthermore, since the assertion that he even tried to achieve a single satiric project in the *Tale*-volume is one that cannot in any case be proved, we must agree again to a fact that is obvious enough anyway: each of the parts may be regarded as, and profitably studied as, an entity in itself. However, since our emphasis in this chapter will be on Swift's book *as a whole,* our principal task is to discover the nature of the contribution that the various parts make to that whole.

II A Tale of a Tub (*Part 1*)

As books go, *A Tale of a Tub* is not big. For example, *Gulliver's Travels* is more than half again as long. But Sir Walter Scott records that Swift, while reading *A Tale of a Tub* many years after its publication, was moved to exclaim: "Good God, what a genius I had when I wrote that book." [10] Nobody could seriously question the justness of the remark. Despite its faults, the book is the work of a genius. Not only is it a brilliant young man's romp, one of the most hilarious in the history of literature; it is also in certain parts an angry, and still relevant, satire.

Little happens in the early pages of the *Tale*. What the reader finds is, first, a list of Treatises "wrote by" the same Author; then, in some editions, "An Analytical Table" (which we may skip, as not Swift's); then, added to the 1710 edition, "An Apology"; then a little "Postscript to the Apology"; then the "Dedication To Lord Somers" (an early demonstration of Swift's great talent for the backhanded compliment); then "The Bookseller To The Reader"; then "the Epistle Dedicatory To Prince Posterity"; and finally "The Preface." But the narrator appears even yet to be in no hurry, for after the "Preface" comes the "Introduction"; and only after this section does the story commence. All in all, there are sixteen parts to the 1704, and seventeen parts to the 1710, edition of this lengthily introduced and oft-interrupted *Tale*.

Only an unreflecting reader could possibly be duped by Swift's tease. Actually, the book gets under way with one of its major themes—the satire on modern learning—on its very first page. There, in the fashion of "modern" scholarship, the author announces his credentials, so to say, for speaking as an authority. He has published nothing; but with great glibness he tells off his list of Treatises "which will be speedily published." This list includes such absurd works as "A general History of Ears," "A modest Defence of the Proceedings of the Rabble. . . ," and so on—eleven in all. This tongue-in-cheek whimsy is followed by the parody, outlined above, of all the elaborate and ridiculous paraphernalia with which we are to assume a truly scholarly work begins.

Though by no means dominant, this sort of impish wit is, happily, pervasive. One deft trick was the use of Thomas Wotton's notes for the 1710 edition of the text, the one now generally used. Wotton had written a reply (*Observations upon The Tale of a Tub*) in opposition to Swift's 1704 *Tale*. So, when the 1710 edition was being prepared for the press, Swift, to get back at his adversary, coolly stole from Wotton's book remarks which Benjamin Tooke, Swift's printer, used as explanatory footnotes.[11] The victim's reactions to this impudence have not been recorded. Swift's point is clear, however: the "learned" book may not have anything at all to say, but it will have lots of prefaces and, of course, many footnotes.

It may be convenient, though I believe not essential, to see a narrator gradually identifying himself in the early pages of the *Tale*-volume; for some very astute readers have found it helpful, especially in the discovery of Swift's many uses of irony, to distinguish in the *Tale*-volume between the real and the purported author. Whether this narrator is the same throughout the *Tale*-volume and whether he is a consistent and fully realized character are matters that we shall briefly consider later. However, it is in the prefatory sections that some readers speak of first meeting the purported "author" (the persona) of the *Tale*-volume. Appearing initially in his own person in "The Epistle Dedicatory To Prince Posterity," he proves to be a Modern who is astonished that any one "should have Assurance in the face of the Sun, to go about persuading Your Highness [Posterity] that our Age is almost wholly illiterate and has hardly produc'd one Writer upon any Subject." Two voices of irony are here completely distinct. The apparent meaning of the passage is voiced by our sincere (though obtuse) narrator; the real meaning, voiced by Swift, says: "Exactly so. Our age has produced hardly one real writer, and certainly none from among your crowd of hackwriters." The same sort of irony appears just a few pages later, when the "author" makes a comment which Swift's voice flatly contradicts: "There is a Person styl'd Dr. B—tl-y [Bentley]," the narrator reports, "who has written near a thousand Pages of immense Erudition, giving a full and true Account of a certain Squabble. . . . He is a Writer of infinite Wit and Humour."

Our narrator has written "Four score and eleven Pamphlets . . . under three Reigns, and for the Service of six and thirty Factions" (see "Introduction" in the *Tale*); and now, in the throes of writing this *Tale*-volume, he resides in a garret. He tells us that "the shrewdest pieces of this treatise were conceived in a garret" ("Preface"); towards the end of the book he reminds us of "the very garret I am now writing in" ("Digression concerning Madness"). In Section VI of the *Tale* he calls himself "a true modern." On the record, then, he appears to be a fairly typical "modern hack writer." When this hack does finally get to his task of telling a tale about a tub, he straightway interrupts with "A Digression concerning Critics." Shortly thereafter, he interrupts again with "A Digression In The Modern Kind" in which he mournfully confesses that "it is lamentable to behold, with what a lazy scorn many of the yawning readers in our age, do now-a-days twirl over forty or fifty pages of preface and dedication (which is the usual modern stint), as if it were so much Latin." This complaint (perfectly applicable to what he is doing!) aired, the author "happily" resumes his subject, "to the infinite satisfaction both of the reader and the author."

But the subject is not resumed for long. Soon comes "A Digression In Praise of Digressions," with a sober (Swift's sardonic) invitation to the "judicious reader" to find a "fitter" place for it, if he can. The digression completed, the narrator remarks upon his "return, with great alacrity" to his tale. Alas, he simply cannot stay with it. He teeters wildly off—though, of course, Swift sees to it that thematically he is still very much "on"—with "A Digression concerning Madness." The behavior of our narrator thus dramatically validates his own thesis: if we will but see it, here indeed, personified in a modern hack writer, is wantonly insane comedy.

III The Battle of the Books

The comic aspects of *A Tale of a Tub* are integral to Swift's attack on false learning. This attack is in turn reinforced in *The Battle of the Books,* particularly by the central episode in that section: the fable of the spider and the bee.

The Battle of the Books is of only slight historical import in a controversy that for a time aroused deep and fierce antagonisms. Something of the nature of this controversy can be realized from a look at one of its famous high points, a few years earlier. On January 27, 1687, Charles Perrault read to the French Academy *"Le siècle de Louis le Grand."* This poem contained such lines as *"Je vois les anciens, sans plier les genous;/Ils sont grands, il est vrais, mais hommes comme nous."* [12] The French poet's words are so entirely reasonable to twentieth-century ears that we are apt to forget how inevitable would be the conflict until this issue was either resolved or ceased to be of serious concern to anybody. In Swift's day, the issue was still of vital importance.

We need no reminder that Swift's part in the controversy does more credit to his heart than to his head. As a philosophic contribution, his share is of no worth, except unintentionally and insofar as his imagery suggests the trivial nature of the quarrel. He sided with the Ancients—and with his patron. At the same time, in real life he knew and admired the writings of Temple, Addison, Arbuthnot, Gay, and Pope—to mention only a few eminent Moderns of his day. It is thus obvious that his concern in this historic quarrel was less to ridicule the Moderns than it was merely to chastise those men who opposed his patron. The truth of this possibility is buttressed by the fact that some of the best fun and most effective ridicule is not particularly relevant to the issue at stake. For example, when Virgil ("the brave Ancient") is about to be engaged in combat and his adversary lifts the visor of his armor, Virgil "suddenly started"; for the visor did not reveal a face. "The Ancient" had to look deep into the cavernous depths of the helmet, which was "nine times too large" for its owner, to locate the tiny head of the man who was offering to do battle with him. Now, the head was that of Dryden, whose famous translation of Virgil had appeared in 1696. Here is laughter, all right. But to call Cousin Dryden a "pinhead" is not to argue seriously for the central thesis to which Swift was supposedly addressing himself. So, too, as Pons observes, the satire on the very first page of the *Battle* is directed not against the Moderns but against "dogs" of all kinds,[13] ancient and modern.

The first page of the *Battle*, like the first page of *Gulliver's Travels*, deserves more attention than it usually gets. Swift writes, "For, to speak in the phrase of writers upon the politics, we may observe in the Republic of Dogs (which, in its original, seems to be an institution of the many), . . . that civil broils arise among them when it happens for one great bone to be seized on by some leading dog. . . ." These words are tremendously significant, for they show that, while Swift was saying one thing, his imagery was sometimes saying something else. Though we cannot for a moment doubt the sincerity of the support he gave to his patron and to the Ancients, his imagery suggests that Swift really cared nothing whatsoever about this sort of quarrel. He was far above, looking down on this "Republic of Dogs." In other words, he unwittingly but quite decisively undercuts his own reasons for supporting the Ancients. "War," as the very first sentence on the first page of the *Battle* insists, "is the child of pride." If this be so, then this particular little war is ridiculous.

Furthermore, his real though unconscious contempt for both sides in the quarrel is beautifully and characteristically wrapped up in the familiar comparison of man to animal. Émile Pons, who has made a special province out of the investigation of this comparison, says that, to Swift, "Humanity is as depraved as the most contemptible kinds of animals (Man is very likely in Swift's later writings to become even worse than these animals.) From now on [Pons is referring to the time when the *Battle* was written] this comparison of Man and Animal is fixed permanently in Swift's imagination. The link between the two is never to be broken. It . . . will remain a constant factor in his work." [14]

Indeed, the symbol is pervasive; but we shall cite only two instances. The first instance shows Swift using the symbol to comment corrosively on Bentley and Wotton. This comment appears towards the end of the *Battle*, where these Moderns are compared to "two mongrel curs, whom native greediness and domestic want provoke and join in partnership, though fearful, nightly to invade the folds of some rich grazier, . . . [They] creep soft and slow. . . , nor dare they bark, . . . but one surveys the region round, while t'other scouts the plain, if haply to discover, at distance from the flock, some carcass half devoured, the refuse of gorged wolves, or ominous ravens."

But the fable of the spider and the bee, the second instance, is the outstanding demonstration of Swift's employment of "*le mythe animal*" in the *Battle*. In this episode, writes Swift, we learn that there once dwelt in the library of St. James's[15] a certain spider, "swollen up to the first magnitude by the destruction of an infinite number of flies." One Friday, into this spider's web flew a bee, who was temporarily entrapped. Having to his own great satisfaction extricated himself, the bee becomes engaged in conversation with the spider, who is understandably quite angry at the damage done to his web:

"A plague split you," said he, "for a giddy son of a whore, . . . Do you think I have nothing else to do, in the devil's name, but to mend and repair after your arse?"
"Good words, friend," said the bee. . . . I'll give you my hand and word to come near your kennel no more."

The conversation between the spider (symbolizing the Moderns in this "Battle") and the bee (the "Ancients") ends with the bee's remark:

"Your inherent portion of dirt does not fail of acquisitions, by sweepings exhaled from below; and one insect furnishes you with a share of poison to destroy another. So that, in short, the question comes all to this—whether is the nobler being of the two, that which, by a lazy contemplation of four inches round, by an overweening pride, feeding and engendering on itself, turns all into excrement and venom, producing nothing at all, but flybane and a cobweb; or that which, by an universal range, with long search, much study, true judgement, and distinction of things, brings home honey and wax."

Aesop, overhearing this debate, makes the comment that reinforces the bee's position and gets to the heart of the matter:

As for us the Ancients, we are content with the bee to pretend to nothing of our own, beyond our wings and our voice, that is to say, our flights and our language. For the rest, whatever we have got, has been by infinite labour and search, and ranging through every corner of nature; the difference is, that, instead of dirt and poison, we have rather chosen to fill our hives with honey and wax, thus furnishing mankind with the two noblest of things, which are sweetness and light.

The bee in this fable is a fairly elegant fellow, no doubt because Swift got him from Temple's essay "Of Poetry" [16] (and Temple probably read of him in Bacon). The dirty, vulgar spider was added by Swift and, because it is used for satiric purposes, evidences Swift's more characteristic employment of the animal, or to be quite literally exact, the insect myth.

Of greater importance here, however, is the fact that the fable of the spider and the bee makes such an unforgettable impact on the reader. This effect is fortunate for, if we consider the whole *Battle* as exposition or as argument, we must see its confusions and inconsistencies. As suggested above, this work does more credit to Swift's heart than to his head. The fact that he had a heart is, of course, a healthy reminder to students who have not read Swift's biography very carefully.[17] Far more significant than this achievement, though, is the fact that the episode of the spider and the bee almost, and quite miraculously, shades out discordant notes and brings wonderfully into focus all the elements that give abiding value to the satire of the *Battle*. Thus the value of the satire remains where, happily, its force has always been strongest anyway. That is, in addition to supporting Sir William Temple by making sport of the Moderns who had attacked him, the *Battle* does make a notable statement about false learning.

Best read, this book satirizes pretense: learning that is false because, though footnotes and prefaces give it a form, it is entirely lacking in substance. So long as learned pomposity, surly pedantry, and sterile scholarship (all mere dirty "webs" of dirty "spiders") still abide here and there, so long as "mongrel curs" continue to haunt our bowers of learning, Swift's comments in the *Battle* and in the digressions of the *Tale* will remain sharply relevant. True learning, Ancient or Modern, "brings home honey and wax"; and it ministers to mankind with "sweetness and light."

IV   A Tale of a Tub (Part 2)

In "An Apology," which is the first sustained prose in the 1710 edition of *A Tale of a Tub*, Swift commented on his dual satiric purpose and also on his method of composition: "The abuses in Religion, he proposed to set forth in the Allegory of the Coats, and the three Brothers, which was to make up the body of the discourse. Those in learning he chose to introduce by way of digressions." The satire on false learning we have already discussed; it remains now to remark upon (1) the "abuses" in religion and (2) the combining of the two satiric themes under a single heading. A discussion of these two issues leads back to *A Tale of a Tub*.

In his Preface, Swift explains the basis for the *Tale*. When threatened by a whale, sailors fling a tub from the ship, "to divert [the whale] from laying violent hands [*sic*] upon the ship." The "ship in danger" is, as the narrator points out, "the commonwealth." The "dangers" were probably restricted, originally, to Swift's idea of the abuses then most current in religion. Later, as previously suggested, these were mortised with passages depicting abuses in learning—a union harmonious enough, at least thematically, if we use Quintana's thesis that the two were, after all, very much alike.[18] In all likelihood Swift had in mind other meanings of "a tale of a tub," common in his times: what people today might call "a tall tale" or "a cock-and-bull story." Also, in Swift's era dissenting preachers, like his own Jack the quack, sometimes stood upon a tub to preach. From this cluster of meanings that Swift may have had at least vaguely in mind, we may construct an appropriately ironic proclamation: "Here is a cock-and-bull story related by a quack for the good of the commonwealth!"

The narrative line which introduces the satire on abuses in religion begins classically, like innumerable other made-up stories: "Once upon a time, . . ." What follows this classic opening line is an allegory about a father (Christ) who had three sons: Peter (the Roman Catholic Church); Martin (the Church of England); and Jack (the various sects of Protestant dissenters). Dying, the father left a will (the New Testament) and a new coat (the Church) for each son. His last commands were that the coats should not be altered and that the brothers should live together "like brethren and friends." From this point on there develops an all too accurate allegory of Christian church history. Just as members of the infant church of the first century were faced almost immediately with the problem of worldliness, of "keeping up with the Joneses," so were the three youthful brothers in the allegory: for example, to keep abreast of their fashionable friends, they want at one time to wear shoulder knots. They consult their father's will to see if they are allowed to decorate their coats in this fashion. The will at no point says anything about so important a matter, so the brothers do not know what they can do. They are saved only by their highly ingenious device of picking out letters in the will, an "S" here, an "H" there, and so on. In no time they have what they want: S,H,O,U,L,D,E,R C,N,O,T,S. The "C" in *CNOTS* will serve very well for the "K," especially since they cannot find a "K." (Apparently Swift has forgotten that he had caused the father to say, just a few pages earlier: "I have also commanded *in my will,* that you should live together in one house like brethren" [my italics].) In any event, "all farther difficulty vanished," the brothers now wear what they want to wear. This perversion of God's Word (their father's will) continues. At the same time, the brothers fall to quarrelling; and, since residence in one house (the one body of Christ) does not content them, they separate. In fact, Peter finally "very fairly kicks" both his brothers out of doors.

The characterization of the three brothers emerges more fully as this narrative doggedly threads its way through the many digressions. Peter, most readers agree, is not a successfully drawn figure.[19] Martin is certainly not a very engaging sort, but he is at least a sensible person. As a Church-of-England man, he is an integral part of that "Commonwealth" which Swift's "tub" was desirous of protecting. It is obvious that the reader is expected to accept him as the sensible middle-of-the-roader, as the good norm from which both Peter and Jack stray. Thus, Swift seems to have been faced with the very familiar Augustan problem of depicting the reasonable and attractive *via media*, which would be Martin's way, and then of showing how uninviting and unintelligent is the way of those, like Peter and Jack, who for one senseless reason or another wander off the track.

This obvious technique Swift did apply effectively in Section VI, in which he distinguishes between the three treatments given to the finery that each of the brothers had added to their coats. Peter (Roman Catholicism) had added so much lace, fringe, and embroidery and so many ribbons and points that "there was hardly a thread of the original coat [the original church] to be seen." He liked it that way. Jack (the Dissenter) so ripped and tore at the added finery that he looked "like a fresh Tenant of Newgate . . . or like a Bawd in her old Velvet-Petticoat." He, in effect, destroyed the coat. Martin, who took the middle course, removed all that he could, the while resolving "in no Case whatsoever, that the Substance of the Stuff should suffer injury." Again, in Section XI, there is the assumption that Martin holds a sensible middle course between two basically similar extremist brothers: "the phrenzy and the spleen of both have the same foundation."

But however, or even if, Swift may initially have intended to proportion his remarks among Peter, Martin, and Jack so that Martin would always be favorably situated in the middle, it is Jack (the Dissenter) who gets most of the attention, who is pursued most ferociously, and who comes most alive—even if only as a caricature. Swift discharges against him the whole tired arsenal of epithets that mankind seemingly never wearies of using to describe its religious minorities. Indeed, they were ancient epithets when Swift picked them up. For example, Ben Jonson, almost a century earlier, had used very much the same arsenal, even then of vintage brand, to attack his Puritan character, Zeal-of-the-land Busy.[20] So Jack it is, Swift says, "whose intellectuals were overturned"; it is Jack who introduced a new deity, "by some called Babel, by others Chaos"; Jack "brayed"; he was "brimful of zeal." In truth, Thackeray's description, in his *The English Humourists of the Eighteenth Century,* of the final chapters of *Gulliver's Travels* applies much more aptly to Swift's Jack: "past all sense of manliness and shame, filthy in word, filthy in thought, furious, raging, obscene."

Professor Quintana suggests[21] that Swift's intention was to subsume under one head the two major satiric themes with which *A Tale of a Tub* (and, I would add, *The Battle of the Books* and *The Mechanical Operation of the Spirit*) are concerned: the satire on false learning and on abuses in religion. Irrationality is the common denominator of both false learning and abuses in religion; irrationality causes both. Swift's central assertion is, therefore, that men will be afflicted with abuses in religion and in learning so long as "fancy gets astride [their] reason" and their "imagination is at cuffs with the senses" (Section IX, *Tale*).

This central theme is most tellingly and formidably stated in Section IX, a "Digression concerning the Original, the Use and Improvement of Madness in a Commonwealth." This digression asks the reader to accept the fantastic premise that man's best recourse is not to his reason, but to madness. From this "commonsensical" first principle Swift proceeds with glaring clarity to examine the real meaning of the serenity accruing to men victimized by delusion:

For the brain in its natural position . . . disposeth its owner to pass his life in the common forms, without any thoughts of subduing multitudes to his own power, his reasons, or his visions; and the more he shapes his understanding by the pattern of human learning, the less he is inclined to form parties after his particular notions, because that instructs him in his private infirmities, as well as in the stubborn ignorance of the people. But when man's fancy gets astride of his reason; when imagination is at cuffs with the senses, and common understanding, as well as common sense, is kicked out of doors; the first proselyte he makes is himself. . . .

. . . .

Those entertainments and pleasures we most value in life are such as dupe and play the wag with the senses. For if we take an examination of what is generally understood by happiness, as it has respect either to the understanding or the senses, we shall find all its properties and adjuncts will herd under this short definition: that it is a perpetual possession of being well deceived.

. . . .

Is any student tearing his straw in piece-meal, swearing and blasheming, biting his grate, foaming at the mouth, and emptying his piss-pot in the spectator's face? Let the right worshipful the commissioners of inspection give him a regiment of dragoons, and send him into Flanders among the rest [of the soldiers].

. . . .

[In Bedlam is a man] gravely taking the dimensions of his kennel, a person of foresight and insight. . . . He walks duly in one pace, entreats your penny with due gravity and ceremony, talks much of hard times, and taxes, and the whore of Babylon, bars up the wooden window of his cell constantly at eight o'clock, dreams of fire, and shoplifters, and court-customers, and privileged places. Now, what a figure would all these acquirements amount to, if the owner were sent into the city among his brethren!

In one sense, these amazing passages from the "Digression concerning Madness" are a devastating piece of self-criticism, the point of which entirely escapes the occasionally eloquent but "well deceived" hack-writer who "wrote" them. Truly, as Martin Price remarks, "It is the special gift of the Tale Teller to be able to reach a damaging conclusion with no discomposure. . . ." [22] The comment, with its emphasis on "the Tale Teller," suggests a conclusion which might be appropriately noted here. It is a reading of the *Tale*-volume, which, though not opposed to the one that I stress, is somewhat different and certainly deserves mention. If insistently pursued, this way of thinking leads to Ronald Paulson's belief that "What Swift is representing in the *Tale* is the general outline of an ideal—the concept of the rounded citizen. . . ." [23]

Irvin Ehrenpreis has agreed: "My only postulate is that behind the book [the *Tale*] stands not a list of philosophical propositions but the idea of a good man." [24]

This thesis can be forcefully supported. It is well-known, for example, that Swift was not favorably disposed to "philosophical propositions"; that he characteristically dealt in specific terms; that, at his best, he always *showed* rather than *stated*. Thus he usually defined reactions viscerally, instead of abstractly. For example, by swooning in revulsion Gulliver showed his attitude toward his wife when she embraced him. Underlying this physical reaction is an unstated idea which Swift trusts the reader to articulate: Gulliver does not like his wife. Likewise, in the *Tale*-volume, Swift is not so much formulating a set of abstract assumptions about abuses in religion and learning as he is showing us what a good person is—and is not. The thesis is attractive, for it adds a welcome dimension to the reading of this book. Nonetheless I should prefer to put the emphasis where Swift said in the "Apology" he intended it to be: on "abuses in Religion" and "Those in Learning." As my remarks in this chapter indicate, I do believe that Swift achieved a large measure of success in his stated intention; in fact, as we see later, he got into difficulty because he achieved more than he intended.

After the "Digression concerning Madness" come "A Farther Digression" (Section X), the return to the religious allegory in Section XI, and the "Conclusion" [25] of the *Tale*. These sections seem distinctly anticlimactic. The prose is occasionally forceful; the expository passages reinforce, and the additional details about Jack again dramatically validate, underlying themes in the great "Digression concerning Madness." But the peak of interest has passed.

The third section of the *Tale*-volume is a relatively short section (about twenty-five pages in a modern text), the full title of which is *A Discourse Concerning the Mechanical Operation of the Spirit. In a Letter to a Friend. A Fragment.* Our modern hack—if we allow him to be the "author" of this, too—is consistent with the insane logic he elsewhere demonstrates when, in the *Fragment*, he proposes to treat upon "Religious Enthusiasm, or launching out the soul, as an Effect of Artifice and Mechanic Operation." The hack's (the narrator's) own words are: "I conceive the methods of this art to be a point of useful knowledge in a very few hands, and which the learned world would gladly be informed." The passage can be taken as a parody of some pompous "mechanic's" report to the Royal Academy of Science, a satiric butt that Swift was to assault gleefully again in Book III of *Gulliver's Travels*.

But *The Mechanical Operation of the Spirit* is more than parody. At the beginning its tone is beguilingly objective and informative. The narrator, characteristically detailed in his instruction, tells how those who would mechanically produce the Spirit "violently strain their eyeballs inward, half closing the lids. . . ." "[A]t first, you can see nothing; but after a short pause a small glimmering light begins to appear, and dance before you. Then, by frequently moving your body up and down, you perceive the vapours to ascend very fast, till you are perfectly dosed and flustered, like one who drinks too much in a morning. Meanwhile the preacher is also at work: he begins a loud hum which pierces you quite through; this is immediately returned by the audience, and you find yourself prompted to imitate them, by a mere spontaneous impulse, without knowing what you do."

The narrator cannot long sustain his objective posture. We soon hear him scold: "I am resolved immediately to weed this error out of mankind." Then, though dissenting Jack (of the *Tale*) is not named, it is Jack (or any other dissenter) who is attacked: "in the language of the spirit, cant and droning supply the place of sense and reason." "Hawking, spitting, and belching, the defects of other men's rhetoric, are the flower, and the figures, and ornaments of his." We then get a hardly relevant "history of fanaticism," which includes the familiar charge that religious zeal and enthusiasm correlate closely with sexuality: "Persons of visionary devotion, either men or women, are, in their complexion, of all others the most amorous." [26]

At its close, the *Mechanical Operation* attempts to retain the fiction, earlier introduced, that it is a letter to a friend: "Pray burn this Letter as soon as it comes to your Hands." The fiction is a conventional one during Swift's era, and we take it too seriously if we say that the device does not here succeed: it hardly ever did. Indeed, it is quite probable that Swift introduced it merely to spoof its absurdity since, as we know, much of his satire had a literary basis. However, it is of more import to note that in this *Mechanical Operation of the Spirit,* and for the last time in the *Tale*-volume, a major theme is chorded. *The Mechanical Operation* tells us that "The first ingredient towards the Art of Canting is a competent share of *inward light."* For a single moment to trust such inward light is an abuse of learning and an abuse of religion. In fact, it is (Swift insisted) madness; therefore, to trust this "inward light" is to set up a predictable result: "a man's fancy gets astride on his reason. . . ." "Imagination is at cuffs with the senses, and common understanding, as well as common sense, is kickt out of doors."

V *Evaluations*

Discerning and knowledgeable students of Swift, having read and reread *A Tale of a Tub, The Battle of the Books,* and *The Mechanical Operation of the Spirit* inevitably say at some time in their lives that this is the best volume that Swift ever wrote. The best part of this best volume is, furthermore, *A Tale of a Tub;* and it is the finest prose satire that Swift ever composed. So the comments go. They are not my comments, however. As prose satire, the *Tale* must stand comparison with *Gulliver's Travels;* and my comment with respect to these two works would be something like Johnson's in his *Life of Pope* when he was manfully trying to adjudicate between the poetry of Dryden and that of Pope. Johnson said: "If the flights of Dryden therefore are higher, Pope continues longer on the wing. If of Dryden's fire the blaze is brighter, of Pope's the heat is more regular and constant." Swift never "flew higher," it seems to me, than he did in his "Digression concerning Madness" in *A Tale of a Tub;* but the *Tale* as a whole does not continue so "long on the wing." Because it sometimes bogs down in merely cerebral wit—readers not uncommonly feel that the digressions are used almost past endurance, for example —the *Tale* has by no means the artistic impact that *Gulliver's Travels* has. An unusually outspoken expression of this point of view appears in Donald Bruce's *Radical Doctor Smollett.* Bruce says, ". . . a more quibbling critic might consider that Swift's prose style, with its hedging mysteriousness, its shuffling archly backwards and forwards, its elaborately concessive manner and its facetious circumstances, resembles nothing more than one of those Chinese carvings from a single piece of ivory in which a fretted globe revolves round a fretted globe containing nothing more than a fretted globe. . . . Surely no joke was ever so ponderously and so protractedly wearisome as the diction of *The Tale of a Tub!*" [27]

There are several other, and I think better, reasons for this type of reaction, and they explain why *Gulliver's Travels* is a more effective and a better book than *A Tale of a Tub* considered separately or the *Tale*-volume viewed as a whole. One obvious reason is that the person of Gulliver gives a relatively consistent point of view to the *Travels*, a quality lacking in the narrator of the *Tale*-volume. Gulliver does for the most part appear to be a "real" narrator. The modern hack of the *Tale*-volume is apparently a useful fiction to so many readers that I have not hesitated to employ him. If he is helpful to readers, that is probably enough. But he should be used with some care, for he is not a consistently convincing character. He need not, in fact, be regarded as a character at all.

Some use is unquestionably made of the persona device, but the "author" of the *Tale*-volume is clearly Jonathan Swift, and not a persona. Too heavy a concern for the supposed narrator, "the modern hack," might perhaps even be somewhat defeating; for much of the delight in confronting this book lies in watching the dazzling performance of a brilliant young man, Jonathan Swift, as he manipulates the materials that constitute the *Tale* and the *Tale*-volume. Swift is the central character of this volume. His brilliance informs it; but he is not so good a narrator as Gulliver because his confusions also inform it. For instance, we can quite reasonably wonder when to stop scoffing at a dissenter's "enthusiasm" (which Swift mercilessly ridicules) and when to begin admiring a judicious admixture of it in a Church-of-England man. After all, as Swift wrote in his *Letter to a Young Gentleman* (1720), "If your Arguments be strong, in God's name offer them in as moving a Manner as the Nature of the Subject will properly admit. . . ."

In other words, as in Book III of *Gulliver's Travels,* the satire of the *Tale*-volume is sometimes more sprayed than aimed. The brutal satire on the sacraments of the Roman Catholic Church is so generalized that it also attacks the Protestant Churches' sacraments of baptism and the Lord's Supper. The resultant ambiguities simply compound Swift's difficulty; for, under the best of conditions, and however ardently a man wants to defend his church and its tenets, he cannot attack the abuses in his own church and the absurdities in other religious sects without some people's mistaking his intention—without some people's thinking he is attacking the Established Church, or even religion itself. It is not surprising, therefore, that Swift's intentions were misunderstood, and legend is almost convincing when it reports the lines attached to the door of St. Patrick's Cathedral, the day Swift was installed as dean:

> Look down, St. Patrick, look, we pray,
> On thine own Church and Steeple;
> Convert thy Dean, on this Great Day;
> Or else God help the People! [28]

Another reason most readers prefer *Gulliver's Travels* to the *Tale*-volume is that Swift's narrative line, at its best in *Gulliver's Travels* (as any child will testify), is weak in the *Tale*-volume. The story is not one to hold children from play and old men from the chimney corner. In fact, only in the spider-bee episode and in certain sections of the history of the three brothers is there very much story at all.

Finally, the *Tale*-volume is more witty than humorous and does not yield anything like the amount of wonderfully uncomplicated joy of *Gulliver's Travels*. We recall, for example, "little" Gulliver taking a flying leap over the dung left by a Brobdingnagian cow. The jump is a failure, for Gulliver falls in "up to my knees." (To say that this funny scene suggests that man's pride leads him to attempts that common sense should teach him to shun is an absurdly pretentious piece of explication.) We recall "little" Gulliver rowing that huge boat in the Brobdingnagian tub, a boat which Glumdalclitch always carried ("when I had done") ". . . into her closet, and hung . . . on a nail to dry." From Book IV we remember the horse races, described as "feats of strength and agility [fair enough]; where the victor is rewarded with a song in his or her praise" [*horses* singing!]. The *Tale*-volume, because it gives us relatively little of this sort of fun, is proportionately a less engaging book than is *Gulliver's Travels.*

In the end, we have to look squarely at the *Tale*-volume itself and attempt some sort of assessment. We can say it is a powerful book, a brilliant book, a clever book, a fascinating book, a disturbing book; and all these judgments would be right. But I believe we must also say that it is a curiously unsatisfactory book.

The greatness of the *Tale*-volume lies in such unforgettable passages as the one in "A Digression concerning Madness," where Swift wrote, "Last week I saw a woman flayed, and you will hardly believe how much it altered her person for the worse." What this passage and the *Tale*-volume as a whole say is that self-deception is avoidable if fancy is not astride reason and if imagination is not at cuffs with the senses. If we flay the rind off, we can see the kernel beneath the rind, the reality beneath appearance; and, even though the reality is not attractive, it is at least discovered for what it is. No man ever stated this truth more powerfully. No one ever so effectively depicted the terrible dangers that must ensue when imagination "gets astride" on reason, and sense yields the reins to fancy. No doubt many reasonable men cherish Swift primarily because he makes this warning unforgettable.

Perhaps, therefore, our gratitude should restrain the easy comment that in Swift's own writings there are elements that are less emphatically and dourly one-sided in their insistence that reason be predominant. We cite only the scores and scores of delightful verses to and for friends, verses brimming with "fancy" and "imagination." And it is even easier to point out—Swift's words, if not his actions to the contrary notwithstanding—that a civilized life depends on reason bedding down in necessary harmony with fancy. It is a kind of madness to insist that one or the other must be forever subjugated. Swift's insistent plea that fancy and imagination must be dominated by reason leads, if too literally heeded, to a sterile, Houyhnhnm-culture in which fun is dead and joy is forever locked outside.

Nonetheless, it must be assumed that Swift gave unquestioned allegiance to this great romantic delusion of the Age of Reason: the concept that Reason would prevail, if we but let it; that Reason ought to prevail, and we should let it. Fancy, this delusion insists, is therefore to be excoriated; Imagination is excommunicated; Reason is alone idealized.

The best explanation of why the *Tale*-volume is not entirely successful may be demonstrated precisely at this point. As critics we are not seriously concerned with the interesting but hardly relevant question of agreement or lack of agreement with the author, however important such a question is. Rather, as I have suggested earlier, the problem is that ambiguities in the book allow for readings that have a disconcerting way of cancelling each other out. For example, Reason cannot be idealized if we accept the very clear implications of the imagery in this little catechism in Section II of the *Tale:* "what is man himself but a micro-coat, or rather a complete suit of clothes with all its trimmings? . . . [T]hose beings, which the world calls improperly suits of clothes, are in reality the most refined species of animals. . . . Is it not they who walk the streets, fill up parliament-, coffee-, play-, bawdy-houses? . . . If one of them is trimmed up with a gold chain, and a red gown, and a white rod, and a great horse, it is called a Lord-Mayor. . . ." We may comment here that Swift does not make much use of this startling image; Carlyle, in *Sartor Resartus,* much more fully explored its possibilities. We ought also to observe, however, that the image, even if little used, does nonetheless say that man's predicament has come about not because his imagination has dominated his reason; rather it has come about because he has no reason at all. He is not even a man. He is more like, if we care to meditate about it, a broomstick: brainless; incapable of thought.

Further, Reason cannot be idealized if, as Section VIII insists, "the original cause of all things . . . be wind, from which principle this whole universe was at first produced." For, "in consequence of this, . . man brings with him into the world, a peculiar portion or grain of wind. . . . This, when blown up to its perfection, ought not to be covetously hoarded up, stifled, or hid under a bushel, but freely communicated to mankind. Upon these reasons, and others of equal weight, the wise Aeolists affirm the gift of BELCHING to be the noblest act of a rational creature." Where is reason if "the original cause of all things. . . . be wind"? It is eliminated.

Again, the imagery in the *Tale*-volume says that men's difficulties result not so much from the absence of Reason as from the presence of a sovereign animality. In the *Tale*, as in the *Battle* and in the *Mechanical Operation*, abundant and inescapable images affirm the equation (man = animal) or imply it: for example, "a true critic . . . is like a dog at a feast" ("Digression concerning Critics"); "Peter . . . [acted] like a well-educated spaniel" (Section IV); "it is with men as with asses; whoever would keep them fast, must find a very good hold at their ears" (Section XI); "he [Jack] had a tongue so musculous and subtile, that he could twist it up into his nose, and deliver a strange kind of speech from thence. He was also the first in three kingdoms, who began to improve the Spanish accomplishment of braying; and having large ears, perpetually exposed and erected, he carried his art to such a perfection, that it was a point of great difficulty to distinguish, either by the view or the sound, between the original and the copy" (Section XI). The imagery continues in the same vein in the famous Section IX of the *Tale* ("Digression concerning Madness") that first takes us into a madhouse and then asks us to "Accost the hole of another kennel[;] first stopping [the] nose, . . . behold a surly, gloomy, nasty, slovenly mortal, raking in his own dung, and dabbling in his urine. The best part of his diet is the reversion of his own ordure, which, expiring into steams, whirls perpetually about, and at last reinfunds."

The animality at the basis of this imagery surely "does more," as Émile Pons remarks, "than depict man as having the features and aspects of an animal"; it does more than "dissociate the 'indivisible' self into animal or mechanical aspects"; [29] the "more" is the fact that the animality precludes the existence of Reason. Thus Pons's comment: "[Swift] undermines all [Reason's] foundations and does not allow it even confidently to deny or doubt.[30] Swift intended, as he said, to write about "abuses in Religion . . . [and] in Learning." What seems to have happened is that, while brilliantly fulfilling this intention, his imagery was too often fulfilling a quite different intention. Thus his imagery seems to articulate the unhappy conviction that the insane world of his "Digression concerning Madness" is in truth the real world; and that this insane world is a world sovereign in animality and therefore devoid of reason. However, to suggest this confusion at the heart of his book is not at all to take from Swift the success he had with his stated intention. The confusion is a flaw of the book and may explain our final dissatisfaction with it, but it cannot allow us to dismiss the book: Swift does expose abuses in religion and learning; he does make us see the dreadful irrationality underlying and causing these abuses. This thesis, so clearly enunciated by Ricardo Quintana, is attractive; and it seems to me still to embrace as much of the *Tale*-volume as any single thesis can embrace this ambiguous and wildly complicated "nest of boxes."

CHAPTER 3

Later Prose of the English Years

I Propagandist and Pamphleteer

IN 1712 Swift was forty-five years old. He had to his credit a small clutch of good poems; he was known as the author of *A Tale of a Tub;* he had written, or was about to write, a number of prose works of great and immediate importance; and he was in England. When the Tories came to power in 1710, "their great difficulty," he wrote in 1714, in his *Memoirs, relating to That Change in the Queen's Ministry in 1710,* "lay in the Want of some good Pen, to keep up the Spirit raised in the People, to assert the Principles, and justify the Proceedings of the new Ministers. . . ."

Swift became the "good pen" that the ministry needed. As the chief journalist for and historian of the Tory party during the last four years of Queen Anne's reign, he was impressively successful. As editor of *The Examiner,* he did great good for his party; in his *Conduct of the Allies* he wrote one of the most successful pieces of party propaganda in journalistic history. The pamphlet sold astronomically well, for those days: eleven thousand copies between its publication on November 27, 1710, and the end of the year, about five weeks later.[1] Swift worked very hard, too, on his *History of the Four Last Years of the Queen*—a book intended to vindicate a Tory ministry for which he had such high hopes; in the service of which he had given so much of himself; and from which, at the end, he got so very little.

Today, *The Examiner, The Conduct of the Allies,* and *The History of the Four Last Years of the Queen* are rarely read since they have slight value as literature. However, some of Swift's poems from this period—poems like "A Description of the Morning," and "A Description of a City Shower," both of which appeared in *The Tatler*—are read of late by increasing numbers and with increasing respect. Present-day readers find delight in *The Journal to Stella,* a product of these years in England. And there is also another of Swift's prose works that is well-known, though hardly ever consulted, that belongs to this period and deserves some comment since it was written with sparkle and a beautiful clarity: the pamphlet *A Proposal for Correcting, Improving and Ascertaining* [stabilizing, or "fixing"] *the English Tongue* (1712).

With respect to the *Proposal,* two assertions are current: the first is that this pamphlet is the only publication that ever appeared under Swift's name; the second, that Swift was wrong in his major thesis. If we may regard his famous epitaph as an exception to the first assertion, since after all, the epitaph appeared after his death, both generalizations are correct. Swift's proposal was, in essence, that the ministry should establish an English Society equivalent to the French Academy and that the English Society be empowered to halt further corruption of the language by permanently "fixing" its parts: "what I have most at Heart," he wrote, "is, that some Method should be thought on for Ascertaining and Fixing our Language for ever, after such Alterations are made in it as shall be thought requisite. For I am of the Opinion, that it is better a Language should not be wholly perfect, than that it should be perpetually changing; and we must give over at one Time or other, or at length infallibly change for the worse." Swift does slightly qualify his position: he does "not mean that [our language] should never be enlarged: Provided, that no Word, which a Society shall give a Sanction to, be afterwards antiquated and exploded, they may have Liberty to receive whatever new ones they shall find Occasion for." Old books will therefore be forever valued for their intrinsic worth: they can always be read, for the words will always be with us.

Swift's antagonist, Richard Bentley, surly pedant that Swift thought him to be, had nonetheless a clearer understanding of the way language behaves. In his *Dissertation Upon Phalaris,* Bentley had written: "Every living language, like the perspiring bodies of living creatures, is in perpetual motion and alteration; some words go off, and become obsolete; others are taken in, and by degrees grow into common use; or the same word is inverted to a new sense and notion, which in tract of time makes as observable a change in the air and features of a language, as age makes in the lines and mien of a face." [2]

Modern linguistic theory is properly impatient with Swift since evidence so overwhelmingly proves that Bentley was right. It is not possible, or even desirable, to halt change in a living language. But Swift's untenable position is at least perfectly consistent with his stand on other matters: he did not like change; he liked reason, order, and wise authority. Since opposition to change in language merely meant, to him, an opposition to corruption in language, his position is entirely understandable. He was a writer and a lover of literature, and so were many of his closest friends. We should expect, therefore, that he would be attracted to what Professor Landa calls "a sanctioned standard language, in order to give permanent life to all written works." [3]

II The Journal to Stella

Among the most interesting of Swift's writings during this time was a group of letters which he wrote to his two spinster friends in Ireland, Esther Johnson and Mrs. Dingley. Though the letters were never addressed solely to Stella, they are grouped under the title *The Journal to Stella* and have been so grouped and so titled since Thomas Sheridan first assembled and published them in the latter part of the eighteenth century. [4]

Swift wrote his first *Journal* entry on September 1, 1710, in Chester, just after he landed in England. His last letter was written in Chester, on June 6, 1713, just before he left England to spend most of his next thirty-five years as Dean of St. Patrick's Cathedral in Dublin. The sixty-five letters which constitute the *Journal* very often read like bulletins that an affectionate cousin or uncle, away on business, might send home to his family. (Swift was forty-three in 1710; Stella was twenty-nine, and Swift had known her since she was about eight; Rebecca Dingley was about forty-four.) Except for a time after 1711—when Swift was ill, terribly busy, or worried about the fate of the Tory ministry—the tone of the letters is usually affectionate. [5]

Swift employed a kind of "family language," using invented terms like "Presto" and "MD"; he is marvellously conversational, as good letter writers generally are; and he presents many details about himself. The letters are also full, but not too full, of details about his work. For example, he tells how he moves among the great ones of his day: "Mr. Harley came out to me, brought me in, and presented me to his son-in-law, lord Doblane (or some such name) and his own son, and, among others, Will Penn the quaker: we sat two hours drinking as good wine as you do; and two hours more he and I alone" (September 30, 1710).[6]

Although he tells about his work, he is usually, and perhaps deliberately, vague as to details. The last line of the passage just quoted illustrates this. Here are some others:

I design to stay here all the next week, to be at leisure by myself, to finish something of weight I have upon my hands. . . . [September 29, 1711].

. . . .

I was this afternoon in the city, eat a bit of meat, and settled some things with a printer [October 18, 1711].

. . . .

I have had a Visiter here that has taken up my time [March 21, 1713].

The rhetorical problem in the situations referred to in these passages was not only to guard against giving away state secrets to spies who intercepted the mails but also, negatively stated, simply to avoid freighting his account with a too heavy load of details about his job. Too much information about routine daily chores would make documentaries out of familiar letters. The special pitch to which Swift tuned for these letters would hardly admit too much of the thick sound of factuality. And that he did have a special tone is indicated by an entry like this one of May 10, 1712: "I have not yet ease or Humor enough to go on *in my Journal Method*" (my italics). The tone itself is sounded in such lines as ". . . methinks you were here and I were prating to you" (January 16, 1711).

Indeed, much of the *Journal* has the tone of a friendly, family-type chat. We seem actually to hear the writer talking conversationally, avuncularly, as though his two dear spinster friends were right there with him:

Methinks I don't write as I should, because I am not in bed: see the ugly wide lines. God almighty ever bless you, etc.

. . . .

Faith, this is a whole treatise; I'll go reckon the lines on t'other side. I've reckoned them [October 12, 1710].

.   .   .   .

. . . and so get you gone to ombre [a card game], and be good girls, and save your money, and be rich against Presto [Swift] comes, and write to me now and then: I am thinking it would be a pretty thing to hear sometimes from sawcy MD [My Dear or My Dears]; but don't hurt your eyes, Stella,[7] I charge you [October 12, 1710]. . . . and am now got into bed, and going to open your letter; and God send I may find MD well, and happy, and merry, and that they love Presto as they do fires. Oh, I won't open it yet! yes I will! no I won't; . . . . What shall I do? My fingers itch; and I now have it in my left hand; and now I'll open it this very moment. . . . Pshaw, 'tis from Sir Andrew Fountain. . . [October 14, 1710].

In other samplings from *The Journal* Swift talks about the writing that he has done or is doing: "This day came out the *Tatler* made up wholly of my *Shower*, and a preface to it. They say 'tis the best thing I ever writ, and I think so too" (October 17, 1710). Or: "I have been 6 hours to day morning writing 19 pages of a Lettr to day to Ld Treasr, about forming a Society or Academy to correct and fix the English Language" (February 21, 1712).

He grumbles about his man-servant, the immortal Patrick: "I have a mind to turn that puppy away: he has been drunk ten times in three weeks. But I han't time to say more; so good night, etc." (October 18, 1710).

He speaks often of his health, or lack of it: "I have left off lady Kerry's bitter, and got another box of pills. I have no fits of giddiness, but only some little disorder towards it; and I walk as much as I can" (February 13, 1711).

He also writes of his hopes for a clerical appointment:

This Morning My Friend Mr. Lewis came to me, and shewed me an Order for a Warrant for the 3 vacant Deanryes, but none of them to me; this was what I always foresaw, and receive the notice of it better I believe than he expected. . . . [A]t Noon Ld Tr hearing, I was in Mr. Lewis's Office, came to me, & sd many things too long to repeat. I told him I had nothing to do but go to Ireld immediately, for I could not with any Reputation stay longer here, unless I had something honorable immediately given to me [April 13, 1713].

And he also gossips: "Odso, I forgot; I thought I had been in London. Mrs. Tisdal is very big, ready to ly down. Her Husband is a puppy" (June 6, 1713).

William Irving, writing about these letters to Stella and Dingley, concludes perceptively, by referring to "the strange picture they leave of Swift as delightful friend, moralist, schoolmaster, and damned soul. . . . The pain of things is there and elsewhere in Swift's letters and gives his whole production a peculiarly Vergilian power over the imagination, till men say that these must be among the great letters of all time." [8] This is very high praise indeed, but I believe we must endorse it.

III   *"The Conclusion, in Which Nothing Is Concluded"*

During these few English years Swift wrote a tremendous amount of prose, much of it narrowly topical. Perhaps we should therefore recall how very selective our chapter is: our attention has as usual been directed to those writings which have transcended the occasions that produced them. With this aim in mind, *A Proposal for Correcting, Improving and Ascertaining the English Tongue,* and *The Journal to Stella* have seemed to me the prose most immediately rewarding to our study, and for that reason we have looked at them rather carefully.

Only one other problem should be noted: this problem is that *The Journal to Stella* just as inevitably raises, as does our chapter on the poetry of Swift, the question of the Swift-Stella relationship. Harold Williams remarks that the "enigmatic relationship" between these two, "a relationship which continued without change on either hand, for thirty years or more, has puzzled every inquirer." [9] No doubt all Swift scholars hope that the truth will someday be known. One of Swift's earliest biographers, John Hawkesworth, concluded that Swift and Stella were married. Hawkesworth then says, ". . . why his marriage was so cautiously concealed, and why he was never known to meet her but in the presence of a third person, are enquiries which no man can answer, without absurdity, and are therefore unprofitable objects of speculation." [10] I do not believe that the force of the last part of Hawkesworth's remark has as yet been sufficiently felt. If it is ever felt, or if the truth is ever known, one obviously tangential but happily immediate benefit will be a cessation of speculation about the problem. Another will perhaps be that some scholars who have heretofore addressed themselves with tremendous cleverness and zeal to the puzzle[11] will turn their fine intelligences to a study of other scholarly and critical problems about which more facts are available. Meanwhile, I believe that our conclusion must be like Samuel Johnson's in *Rasselas*, a "conclusion, in which nothing is concluded." However, the reader who wishes to pursue this particular problem would be best advised to begin by consulting Maxwell B. Gold's *Swift's Marriage to Stella*. Though committed to a thesis (Swift and Stella were married), Mr. Gold's systematic assembling of all the known evidence is a most useful introduction.

CHAPTER 4

The Left-handed Poet

IN middle age, Swift referred to himself as one who ". . . had the Sin of Wit no venial Crime; Nay, 'twas affirm'd, he sometimes dealt in Rhime; Humour, and Mirth, had Place in all he writ" ("The Author Upon Himself, 1714"). If Swift was not quite accurate, "Humour and Mirth" do inform a great deal, if by no means all, of his poetry; and in his comment that he "sometimes dealt in Rhime," he is guilty only of hugely understating the facts. Though to my knowledge no one has counted lines to prove this point, it is probably safe to say that in the Augustan Age only Swift's young friend Alexander Pope wrote more poetry than Swift. Also, Pope generally wrote better poetry and was more careful of his literary estate; much of Swift's poetry moved rather accidentally into the public domain.[1]

Swift's early poetry usually does not get much comment. For one thing, most readers think that the later poetry is better and more interesting. Moreover, except to scholars, these early poems seem so little "Swiftean." The bases for these criticisms can perhaps be suggested by a look at Swift's first published poem, the "Ode to the Athenian Society" (1692) in which we find lines of such irremedial flatness as "No sooner does she land/On the delightful Strand/When strait she sees the Countrey all around."[2] We also confront a nearly unbelievable (for Swift) rhetorical posture reflected in these lines: "But as for poor contented me,/ Who must my weakness and my ignorance confess. . . ."

The occasional doggerel and the false posturing of this and of the other early poems have sometimes prompted the hope that their uncommonly sensible maker could have joined most of the rest of the world in willingly letting them die. Such an attitude is unfortunate, for the early poems are of undeniable interest as revealing autobiographical documents;[3] they do interestingly shadow forth themes of major import in the later works;[4] and they are, as Professor Quintana with seraphic charity remarks about Swift's three Pindaric odes, "by no means the worst of their kind."[5] But such facts cannot for any reader make good poems out of mediocre ones.

Though Swift started out seriously enough to be a poet,[6] he began—as is the fashion sometimes with young writers—by imitating men he admired: Abraham Cowley ("when I writt what pleases me I am Cowley to my self"[7]) and his patron, Sir William Temple ("I prefer him to all others at present in England"[8]). Since their gait, so to say, was not his, the results were predictably disappointing: the early poems often read too much like a-young-poet-imitating-somebody-else.

However, the "Ode to the Athenian Society" does raise one of the more interesting biographical questions, for it is still widely believed to have inspired the comment from John Dryden, "Cousin Swift, you will never be a poet." Where Samuel Johnson, the source for this wonderfully quotable sentence and anecdote, got his information, nobody knows. An earlier, more credible, but duller version of the same anecdote appeared in Colley Cibber's *Lives of the Poets* (1753); in it Dryden is reported to have remarked, "Cousin Swift, turn your thoughts some other way, for nature has never formed you for a Pindaric poet." Since Cibber is vague about the source of his information, this story may be merely another of the many fables that have stubbornly barnacled themselves to biographies of Swift.[9] At any rate, if it were not Dryden, who or what did cause young Swift's muse to stop, to pause, and then to start off on a different track?

In a 1693 poem, "Occasioned by Sir W[illiam] T[emple]'s Late Illness and Recovery," Swift addresses his poetic muse as "Malignant goddes! bane to my repose,/ Thou universal cause of all my woes"; and he concludes the poem with words that signal the end of his profitless infatuation:

> I here renounce thy visionary pow'r;
> And since thy essense on my breath depends,
> Thus with a puff the whole delusion ends.

We can only speculate as to the reason, or reasons, for this "renunciation." It perhaps ought to be taken as no more painful to

Swift than Huck Finn's renunciation of persimmons: he didn't like them anyway. Perhaps Swift simply began to be caught up in other matters of more practical concern to his career. Or, finally, after being for a time side-tracked by Sir William Temple's influence,[10] Swift merely returned to the predominantly satiric style that was native to his earlier days. We recall that he had memorized Samuel Butler's *Hudibras*, the famous satire on the Puritans. And Herbert Davis refers to the fact that, in Swift's undergraduate commonplace book, he had copied out verses that clearly indicated a taste for "satire and buffoonery and occasional poems concerned with public affairs." Such activity truly reflects what Professor Davis calls "an early indication of Swift's natural bent." [11]

Swift's "natural bent" gets its best poetic expression in his later poetry. The later poetry is also the most interesting and the most worthy of study, for only in it does Swift sometimes deserve to be called a poet. Ricardo Quintana marks the beginning of this period with the comment that Swift "was no longer an immature writer when, perhaps in 1698, he composed the poem entitled *Verses wrote in a Lady's Ivory Table-Book*. From that moment on he was at home in verse of a kind which answered in its fashion to [his] satiric idiom. . . ." [12] In fact, of course, most of Swift's poetry, satiric and otherwise, was written much "later" then 1698. Joseph Horrell reminds us that Swift "reached his fiftieth birthday having written only one-fifth the poetry he was to write." [13] (He was fifty years old in 1717.) It is to some of these later poems that we now direct our attention.

I A City Shower

One of Swift's best poems, written in 1710, is "A Description of a City Shower":

> Careful Observers may fortel the Hour
> (By sure Prognosticks) when to dread a Show'r:
> While Rain depends, the pensive Cat gives o'er
> Her Frolicks, and pursues her tail no more.
> Returning Home at Night, you'll find the Sink
> Strike your offended Sense with double Stink.
> If you be wise, then go not far to Dine,
> You'll spend in Coach-hire more than save in Wine.
> A coming Show'r your shooting Corns presage,

Old aches [two syllables!] throb, your hollow Tooth will rage.
Sauntring in Coffee-house is Dulman seen;
He damns the Climate, and complains of Spleen.
Mean while the South rising with dabbled Wings
A Sable Cloud a-thwart the Welkin flings,
That swill'd more Liquor than it could contain,
And like a Drunkard gives it up again.
Brisk Susan whips her Linen from the Rope,
While the first drizzling Show'r is born aslope,
Such is that Sprinkling which some careless Quean
Flirts on you from her Mop, but not so clean.
You fly, invoke the Gods; then turning, stop
To rail; she singing, still whirls on her Mop.
Not yet, the Dust had shun'd th' unequal Strife,
But aided by the Wind, fought still for Life;
And wafted with its Foe by violent Gust,
'Twas doubtful which was Rain, and which was Dust,
Ah! where must needy Poet seek for Aid,
When Dust and Rain at once his Coat invade;
His only Coat, where Dust confus'd with Rain,
Roughen the Nap, and leave a mingled Stain.

．　 ．　 ．　 ．　 ．　 ．　 ．　 ．　 ．

　Now from all Parts the swelling Kennels [gutters] flow,
And bear their Trophies with them as they go:
Filth of all Hues and Odours seem to tell
What Street they sail'd from, by their Sight and Smell.
They, as each Torrent drives, with rapid Force
From Smithfield, or St. Pulchre's shape their Course,
And in huge Confluent join at Snow-Hill Ridge,
Fall from the Conduit prone to Holborn-Bridge.
Sweepings from Butchers Stalls, Dung, Guts, and Blood,
Drown'd Puppies, Stinking Sprats, all drench'd in Mud,
Dead Cats and Turnip-Tops come tumbling down the Flood. (1710)

　The poem exhibits considerable skill. First, we should note the antipoetic diction. Swift deliberately parodies both the vocabulary and the metaphors of "polite" conversation ("the South rising with Dabbled Wings") with "A Sable Cloud a-thwart the Welkin flings/ That swill'd more Liquor than it could contain/ And like a Drunkard gives it up again." Or better yet, we should note the "Drown'd Puppies," "stinking Sprats," "Dead Cats," and "Turnip-tops" of the last stanza. "Here," Swift seems to be saying, "if we must describe a City Shower, let us describe it *as it is.*" Second, the lines are held tight by the frequent alliteration, of which Swift was fond ("Strike your offended Sense with double Stink"), and the characteristically abundant internal rhyme and assonance ("While Rain depends, the pensive Cat gives o'er"; "Old Aches throb, your hollow Tooth will rage"). Third, we should consider the rhyme and rhythm. To be sure, the last three lines are a triplet (*Blood-Mud-Flood*), ending with an Alexandrine (a six-stress line). But elsewhere in the poem the rhymes are doublets (*aa/bb/cc/dd/*, etc.), and the rhythm is prevailing five stresses per line. Most of Swift's poetry is written in a four-beat line of eight syllables (iambic tetrameter). In all other important respects, however, this poem is characteristic of Swift's best poetry.

Patricia Spacks notes that the concluding lines of "A Description of a City Shower" "provide a more forceful indictment of the disorder and filth of the city than could be achieved by ten times their bulk in moral or sociological comment." [14] Maybe so, but I suspect that Swift would be surprised to hear such talk. I believe the more relevant comments should refer to the temperamental and literary basis of the satire in this poem. For, always an anti-romantic, Swift would insist that the unpleasant facts about a shower should not be glossed over. We should see it as it is,[15] and that means to see it as he sees it. Also, Swift's satire very often had a literary basis, as it has here. What he ridicules is the unreal language, the affectations, the elegant absurdities of "fashionable" poetry. He preferred, instead, such lines as the following, in this poem of 1710: "Dead Cats and Turnip-Tops come tumbling down the Flood." The same sort of preference is revealed in 1718, with "My master is a parsonable man, and not a spindle-shank'd hoddy-doddy" (from "Mary [Swift's cook] the Cook-Maid's Letter to Dr. Sheridan"); and again in 1733, for example, with "Sit still, and swallow down your spittle" ("On Poetry: A Rapsody").

II *Poems to Stella*

Another of Swift's poems worthy of consideration is "Stella's Birth-day":

All Travellers at first incline
Where'e'er they see the fairest Sign,
And if they find the Chambers neat,
And like the Liquor and the Meat
Will call again and recommend
The Angel-Inn to ev'ry Friend:
And though the Painting grows decayd
The House will never loose it's Trade;

.   .   .   .

Now, this is Stella's Case in Fact:
An Angel's Face, a little crack't;
(Could Poets or could Painters fix
How Angels look at thirty six?)
This drew us in at first to find
In such a Form an Angel's Mind

.   .   .   .

Then Cloe, still go on to prate
Of thirty six, and thirty eight;
Pursue thy Trade of Scandall picking,
Thy Hints that Stella is no Chickin,
Your Innuendo's when you tell us
That Stella loves to talk with Fellows
But let me warn thee to believe
A Truth for which thy Soul should grieve,
That, should you live to see the Day
When Stella's Locks must all be grey
When Age must print a furrow'd Trace
On ev'ry Feature of her Face;
Though you and all your senceless Tribe
Could Art or Time or Nature bribe
To make you look like Beauty's Queen
And hold for ever at fifteen.
No Bloom of Youth can ever blind
The Cracks and Wrinckles of your Mind,
All Men of Sense will pass your Dore
And crowd to Stella's at fourscore. (1721)

Swift wrote eleven poems to Stella, and of these seven were
birthday poems. The birthday present given to her in 1721—long
selections from this poem are reprinted above—is one of the most
engaging of them all. It exhibits many of Swift's characteristic poetic devices: the four-stress line; the *aa/bb/cc/* rhyme scheme;

the frequent alliteration and assonance; the diction, almost always at "middle level," and as studiously unelevated as the author could make it; the marvelous ability (Pope had it also) to confine to the couplet-form both the sense and the intonation of ordinary talk. This birthday poem to Stella also reveals familiar Swiftean touchstones like the preeminent importance of mind and the necessity for getting beneath the mere appearance of things. The poem is characterized, finally, by the teasing but beautiful tenderness in Swift's attitude toward this remarkable woman. She transcribed for publication many of Swift's poems, and I cannot suppose that in this instance she found the chore a dull one. Besides, she was not thirty-six, or even thirty-eight, as the poem states; she was all of forty and must have been grateful for Swift's customary carelessness with dates.

As with *The Journal to Stella,* a by no means incidental point is the "evidence" that this and other birthday poems add to the much-mooted question of the Swift-Stella marriage, or lack of it. The "evidence" is obviously subjective. Nonetheless, there is certainly some truth in Ricardo Quintana's remark that, "If there is anywhere a key to the enigmatic relations between Swift and Stella, it lies in these extraordinary occasional pieces." [16] Unfortunately, the way this "key" is used is likely to reveal more about the critic than about Swift and Stella. Nonetheless, I must offer my conviction that these poems to Stella ("no chicken" she) are not love poems. They do not say anything about a marriage. However, I think they do say that Swift never crossed, with Stella, the thin line, miles wide, between tenderness and ardor. A fondly teasing tone is by no means inimical (in fact, may contribute?) to a romantic attachment; but the attachment cannot be based on this tone alone. There has to be something more. Such lines as, "And though the Painting grows decayd/ The House will never loose it's trade" and "Now this is Stella's Case in Fact;/ An Angel's Face, a little crack't" reveal the fondly teasing tone. But no lines in the poem reveal anything more than this.

III *Poems for Fun*

We are on safer ground when we look at another type of poetry. Swift very often versified for fun; and, since this aspect of his poetry deserves illustration, I have from a large store selected, and will present without comment, three samples. He called them "family trifles." [17]

[*No Title*]
      As Thomas was cudgelld one day by his Wife,
      He took to the Street, and fled for his Life,
      Tom's three dearest Friends came by in the Squabble,
      And sav'd him at once from the Shrew and the Rabble;
      Then ventur'd to give him some sober Advice,
      But Tom is a Person of Honor so nice,
      Too wise to take Council, too proud to take Warning,
      That he sent to all three a Challenge next morning.
      Three Duels he fought, thrice ventur'd his Life
      Went home, and was cudgell'd again by his Wife. (?1723)

The Servant's Maxim
            Eat like a Turk
               Sleep like a Dormouse;
            Be last at Work,
               At Victuals foremost. (1725)

Written by the Reverend Dr. Swift
On his own Deafness.
            Deaf, giddy, helpless, left alone,
            To all my Friends a Burthen grown,
            No more I hear my Church's Bell,
            Than if it rang out for my Knell:
            At Thunder now no more I start,
            Than at the Rumbling of a Cart:
            Nay, what's incredible, alack!
            I hardly hear a Woman's Clack. (1734)

IV "*Never any one Liveing thought like you*"

One poem, "Cadenus and Vanessa," "regarded by some as the finest of Swift's metrical pieces," [18] is too long to quote more than excerpts from. The poem gives a sad sort of immortality to Esther Vanhomrigh, the young London lady who fell in love with Swift. Written for her in 1713, and probably revised later, the poem was not published until 1726, three years after her death. When he wrote the poem, Swift ("Cadenus") was in the middle forties, and Esther ("Vanessa") in her early twenties (she was born in 1687 or 1688). The relationship had become complicated when Vanessa indicated that her happiness required the newly appointed Dean of St. Patrick's to change his role from mentor and family friend, which he had been, to lover. Swift was "at an age," wrote Samuel Johnson, "when vanity is strongly excited by the amorous attention of a young woman." [19] The remark may have some truth in it; in any event, Swift appears to have been neither skillful nor kind in the way he handled the love of Miss Vanhomrigh. "Cadenus and Vanessa" begins like a true pastoral:

> The Shepherds and the Nymphs were seen
> Pleading before the Cyprian Queen.
> The Council for the Fair began,
> Accusing that false Creature, Man.

The real intention of this pastoral soon becomes clear. As Professor Quintana says, the purpose is to smooth over an awkward situation by resolving "all difficulties into high comedy." [20] Swift (Cadenus = *Decanus* [Latin for *Dean*]) speaks in his own person:

> Vanessa, not in Years a Score,
> Dreams of a Gown of forty-four;
> Imaginary Charms can find,
> In Eyes with Reading almost blind;
> Cadenus now no more appears
> Declin'd in Health, advanc'd in Years.
> She fancies Musick in his Tongue,
> Nor further looks, but thinks him young.
> What Mariner is not afraid,
> To venture in a Ship decay'd?
> What Planter will attempt to yoke
> A Sapling with a falling Oak?

The advice is sensible, but the tone of the lines vitiates their sense. Where the situation probably called for a certain amount of clearheaded ruthlessness on Swift's part, it received only the arch raillery of "high comedy."

Another stanza refers to Vanessa's pursuit of her Dean:

But what Success Vanassa met,
Is to the World a Secret yet:
Whether the Nymph, to please her Swain,
Talks in a high Romantick Strain;
Or whether he at last descends
To like with less Seraphick Ends;
Or, to compound the Business, whether
They temper Love and Books together;
Must never to Mankind be told,
Nor shall the conscious Muse unfold.

The Queen of Love finally adjudicates this ambiguous and perplexing case: she "Decreed the Cause against the Men." It is not
clear exactly what her decree amounted to; perhaps she should
have been more specific and decreed against "the Man" named
Swift. Samuel Johnson's censure seems to me to be in this instance
not unfair: "[R]ecourse must be had to that extenuation which
[Swift] so much despised, 'men are but men': . . . [N]o other
honest plea can be found, that he delayed a disagreeable discovery from time to time, dreading the immediate bursts of distress,
and watching for a favorable moment." [21] But there is no convincing evidence that a "favorable moment" was in truth ever found,
for Vanessa followed her dean to Ireland where she lingered and
languished, "baffled and embittered," [22] until her death in 1723.
Even before her death, moreover, the relationship between them
had for some reason ended.

The rupture occurred in the summer of 1722,[23] but the reason
for the break must be added to the list of mysteries surrounding
Swift's life. Something of the mystery and much of the bitterness
and bafflement of this tragic story is dramatically illustrated by
one of Esther Vanhomrigh's letters to Swift, about two years before her death: ". . . how many letters must I send you," she
asked, "before I shall receive an answer can you deny me in my
misery the only comfort which I can expect at present oh that I
could hope to see you here . . . I was born with violent passions
which terminate all in one that unexpressible passion I have for
you consider the killing emotions which I feel from your neglect of
me and shew some tenderness for me or I shall lose my senses
. . . I firmly believe could I know your thoughts (which no humane creature is capable of geussing [sic] at because never any

one liveing thought like you) I should find you have often in a rage wished me religious hopeing then I should have paid my devotions to heaven but that would not spair you for was I an Enthusiast still you'd be the Deity I should worship. . . ." [24]

That manuscript copies of Swift's poem to Vanessa must have been in circulation for years before the poem was published is indicated by Swift's letter to Knightley Chetwode (April 19, 1726), in which he said, "I am very indifferent what is done with ["Cadenus and Vanessa"], for printing cannot make it more common than it is." [25] Nothing can tell us whether the "indifference" was real, easily assumed, or painfully forced. We must conclude, therefore, that "Cadenus and Vanessa" remains a tantalizing and ambiguous human document, whatever a reader thinks of it as poetry. (I like Joseph Horrell's comment: the poem is "an elegant piece of persiflage.") [26]

The pastoral cast of "Cadenus and Vanessa" seems to me significant: there is a strong likelihood that Swift was hiding behind it. The unhappy drama which the poem depicts might not have ended tragically if Swift had dealt as openly and as realistically with the real-life "swain" (himself) and the living "nymph" (Miss Vanhomrigh) as he dealt with Dermot and Sheelah in another of his poems, the "Pastoral Dialogue" of 1729. In this lively spoofing of the pastoral tradition, an older—and I would say in this instance a wiser—Swift begins, tongue in cheek: "Sing heavenly Muse in sweetly flowing Strain,/ The soft Endearments of the Nymph and Swain." As the two lovers peel potatoes together, Dermot is moved to express himself as follows:

> When you saw Tady at Long-bullets play,
> You sat and lows'd him all the Sun-shine Day.
> How could you, Sheelah, listen to his Tales,
> Or crack such Lice as his betwixt your Nails?

Sheelah replies:

> When you with Oonah stood behind a Ditch,
> I peept, and saw you kiss the dirty Bitch.
> Dermot, how could you touch those nasty Sluts!
> I almost wisht this Spud were in your Guts.

Dermot extricates himself: ". . . if I ever touch [Oonah's] Lips again,/ May I be doom'd for Life to weed in Rain." And all ends happily with Dermot's passionate declaration: "O, could I earn for thee, my lovely Lass/ A pair of Brogues to bear thee dry to Mass!" Altogether, the conversation bespeaks an attachment which, though stormy, was yet honest. What needed to be said was said; thus the relationship was less calculated inevitably to produce heartache than the real-life counterpart so elegantly obfuscated in "Cadenus and Vanessa."

V *Lampoons*

In 1816 in his *Edinburgh Review* the Scottish critic, Francis Jeffrey, said of Swift: "He was, without exception, the greatest and most efficient *libeller* that ever exercised the trade; and possessed, in an eminent degree, all the qualifications which it requires:—a clear head—a cold heart—a vindictive temper— . . . and a complete familiarity with every thing that is low, homely, and familiar in language." [27] Jeffrey was perhaps a trifle severe, but it is true that Swift was a truly great hater and that he wrote a number of outspoken and sometimes quite cruel verse lampoons. Targets might be George II himself, or Prime Minister Sir Robert Walpole; they might be a great English general, or merely some Irish Yahoos (See "The Legion Club") who were not behaving themselves, politically. The range is wide. How vicious Swift could be is well illustrated by his "Satirical Elegy On the Death of a late Famous General." This poem is Swift's biting *requiescat in pace* to the great Whig general, the Duke of Marlborough.

> His Grace! impossible! what dead!
> Of old age too, and in his bed!
> And could that Mighty Warrior fall?
> And so inglorious, after all!
>
> .   .   .   .
>
> And could he be indeed so old
> As by the news-papers we're told?
> Threescore, I think, is pretty high;
> 'Twas time in conscience he should die.
> This world he cumber'd long enough;
> He burnt his candle to the snuff;

And that's the reason, some folks think,
He left behind so great a s[tin]k.

.   .   .   .

Let pride be taught by this rebuke,
How very mean a thing's a Duke;
From all his ill-got honours flung,
Turn'd to that dirt from whence he sprung. (1722)

Because Swift was himself so much in his writings—in contrast to the esthetic distance maintained by Pope—his critics often confine their comments exclusively to him and say nothing about the poem or prose passage in question. We may recall, as illustration, Thackeray's notorious lines: "Would you have liked to be a friend of the great Dean? . . . If you had been his inferior in parts. . . , he would have bullied, scorned, and insulted you; if, undeterred by his great reputation, you had met him like a man, he would have quailed before you, . . . and years after written a foul epigram about you—watched for you in a sewer, and come out to assail you with a coward's blow and a dirty bludgeon. . . ." [28] This sort of criticism that attacks Swift as a man is really a kind of commentary on the power of what he wrote. Thus, though it must be admitted that the "Satirical Elegy" on Marlborough is, as Harold Williams says, an "ungenerous attack," [29] the comment is relevant as criticism only insofar as it reflects a measure of the tremendous power of the poem. I suspect that what Harold Williams felt was the same sort of impact that most readers must feel: from the first to the last line, with the terrible word, *dirt*, this poem is a statement that, for concentrated venom and pure vindictiveness, is as lethal as anything in the English language. Though we need not cherish the poem for this reason, I believe we should respect it. It brilliantly achieves what its author intended it to achieve.

VI   *The "Unprintable" Poems*

Swift wrote other poems, heretofore usually classified under such uninviting rubrics as "unprintable." Professor Maurice Johnson remarks that "Even the most dispassionate modern critics have called these poems nasty, noxious, disgusting, and painful, and have hastened past with eyes averted." [30] But tastes do change. Professor Johnson thinks highly, and I believe rightly, of an "unprintable" poem like "Strephon and Chloe" (1731). Freer winds are blowing these days, happily, so perhaps this hilariously funny and very wise comment on marriage ("On Sense and Wit your Passion found") may yet receive more attention. Moreover, poems like "The Lady's Dressing Room" (1730) or "A Beautiful Young Nymph Going to Bed" (1731) may now begin to be less frequently shrugged off, as being merely scatological, and receive the serious attention they merit. Swift in these last two poems adopted a device better known from its appearance in Book II of *Gulliver's Travels:* in the boudoir of a female, or group of females, he set a loose-tongued narrator (like Gulliver among the Brobdingnagian ladies-in-waiting) who later told everybody, everything. This "everything" could sometimes be quite offensive; an instance is recorded by Swift's friend, Mrs. Pilkington, who wrote that her old mother threw up her dinner when she heard "The Lady's Dressing Room." [31]

Swift's device was monstrously unfair to the ladies. But his point is clear enough: he simply did not believe in nymphs. "Here," he seems to be saying, "if we must describe women, describe them honestly, as they are." That is, as he writes in "To Stella" (1720),

> . . . should a Porter make Enquiries
> For Chloe, Sylvia, Phillis, Iris;
> Be told the Lodging, Lane, and Sign,
> The Bow'rs that hold those Nymphs divine;
> Fair Chloe would perhaps be found
> With Footmen tippling under Ground,
> The charming Silvia beating Flax,
> Her Shoulders mark'd with bloody Tracks;
> Bright Phillis mending ragged Smocks,
> And radiant Iris in the Pox.

The intention to record reality aright is laudable, even if the insistence that facts usually ignored must be considered led paradoxically to unreality. When facts usually ignored become *the* picture, instead of *part* of a picture, distortion is inevitable. Moreover, when exaggeration is combined with distortion, the result is caricature, which can be very funny. Swift's "Beautiful Young

Nymph" is caricature, but it is not funny; and it is not funny
mainly because Swift feels so strongly both that what he sees is
the terribly real whole truth of this situation, and that this whole
truth is quite horrible to contemplate. Had these lines from the
"Beautiful Young Nymph" been read to Mrs. Pilkington's mother,
I have no doubt that she would have had to throw up again:

> Corinna, Pride of Drury-Lane,
> For whom no Shepherd sighs in vain;
> Never did Covent Garden boast
> So bright a batter'd, strolling Toast;
> No drunken Rake to pick her up,
> No Cellar where on Tick to sup;
> Returning at the Midnight Hour;
> Four Stories climbing to her Bow'r;
> Then, seated on a three-legg'd Chair,
> Takes off her artificial Hair:
> Now, picking out a Crystal Eye,
> She wipes it clean, and lays it by.
> Her Eye-Brows from a Mouse's Hyde,
> Stuck on with Art on either Side,
> Pulls off with Care, and first displays 'em.
> Then in a Play-Book smoothly lays 'em.

And so on and so on. The poem is truly wonderful and entirely
relentless, both as parody of the too familiar "poetic" depiction of
a "nymph" and as a limning of a filthy female. The degree of distortion in this caricature is sharply illuminated if we recall John
Donne's management of much the same situation in his "To His
Mistris Going to Bed":

> Off with that girdle, like heavens Zone glistering,
> But a far fairer world incompassing.
> Unpin that spangled breastplate which you wear,
> That th'eyes of busie fooles may be stopt there.
>
> . . . .
>
> Full nakedness! All joyes are due to thee,
> As souls unbodied, bodies uncloth'd must be,
> To taste whole joyes. Gems which you women use
> Are like Atlanta's balls, cast in mens views,
> That when a fools eye lighteth on a Gem,
> His earthly soul may covet theirs, not them.

[75]

Swift's Corinna has a different look about her. She "Pulls out the rags contriv'd to prop/ Her flabby dugs, and down they drop."

> Up goes her Hand, and off she slips
> The Bolsters, that supply her Hips.
> With gentlest Touch, she next explores
> Her Chancres, Issues, running Sores.

The poem ends with these lines: "The nymph, though in this mangled plight,/ Must ev'ry morn her limbs unite./ . . . Who sees will spew; who smells be poisoned." If the last line had read, "Who sees *should* spew," then the depiction of this poor prostitute would have led us finally to, and in fact invited, moral censure.[32] It might even have allowed some pity. It does not, for here is the fact: Who sees this nymph "will spew."

The poem contrasts instructively not only with Donne's "To His Mistris Going to Bed," but also with Pope's "The Rape of the Lock." Pope's Belinda is of a higher social level, but morally she is on a par with the Corinna of Swift's poem. The significant differences, however, are in the points of view and in the methods of the two poets. Pope is far more the craftsman and far more the poet. His Belinda, getting ready for the day, "Repairs her smiles," "awakens every grace," and—as she continues with her makeup —"Sees by degrees a purer blush arise." Working here for Pope is a brilliant and a believable metaphor: Belinda is like any fashionable belle; she is restored to herself by what she puts on. The metaphor shapes all the lovely innuendoes of this passage. As an objective observer, Pope saw that what Belinda put on was by no means, after all, quite so important as she thought it to be; but this he realized with a sardonic and and even a kindly tolerance.

Swift, on the other hand, was not an objective observer. In the "Beautiful Young Nymph" he is not kind and he is not tolerant, and because, to borrow two useful phrases from T. S. Eliot's *After Strange Gods*, the "man who suffers" is rarely separate in this or in any of Swift's poems from the "mind that creates," the result is that the man Swift is always in his poems, caring very much that we understand what he sees and thinks and caring also very much that we understand what we ought to see and think. Because he cared so much, he was compellingly insistent that we wipe off Corinna's greasy façade and see her for the dreadful bawd that she is. This concern was so very urgent that he could not be objective, he could not be kind, and he was even forced into exaggeration (Surely no such "heroine" as Corinna ever lived!).

Further, the figurative language of metaphor and symbol is used only in the most obvious sense in the "Beautiful Young Nymph," as in Swift's poems generally; and it is never used as a shaping principle for the whole poem (as Pope used it, with Belinda; or Swift himself, with the Lilliputians in *Gulliver's Travels*). Thus the "Beautiful Young Nymph" is typical of Swift's poetry in that it is more glaringly photographic than generative. This poem is, therefore, memorable only as a statement about a squalid, dirty whore. It is so strong as statement that I should like to insist that it is memorable. Unlike "The Rape of the Lock," however, it is not a splendidly and continually unfolding metaphor; rather, it is a photograph whose limitations and distortions —and power—are explained by the fact that it was taken through a keyhole, by a Peeping Tom (the Reverend Jonathan Swift, D.D.), who was morally outraged by what he saw.

VII *Poetry as Talk*

One final aspect of Swift's poetry deserves more explicit comment. Again like Pope, Swift had a great talent (referred to above) for re-creating dialogue. Maurice Johnson makes a fine comment about this: "What there is to grin at in Swift's poetry often arises from characterization through monologue and dialogue ingeniously adapted to rhyme. His cookmaids, noblemen, idle wives, clergymen, bookdealers, and politicians speak unmistakably in voices of their own. They ramble or superciliously condescend, gabble, or protest in turn."[33]

A good illustration of this talent may be found in one of those poems—all of them are of considerable interest—in which Swift writes about himself: "Verses on the Death of Dr. Swift" (1731). In the following grimly ironic excerpt (Who but Swift would think to write humorous verses about his own death?), he has set down some conjectures about the reactions of the gentler sex to the author's (Swift's) demise. The ladies are at the card table:

My female Friends, whose tender Hearts
Have better learn'd to act their Parts,
Receive the News in doleful Dumps,
"The Dean is dead, (and what is Trumps?)
"Then Lord have Mercy on his Soul.
"(Ladies I'll venture for the Vole.)
"Six Deans they say must bear the Pall.
"(I wish I knew what King to call.)
"Madam, your Husband will attend
"The Funeral of so good a Friend.
"No Madam, 'tis a shocking Sight,
"And he's engag'd Tomorrow Night!
"My Lady Club wou'd take it ill,
"If he shou'd fail her at Quadrill.
"He lov'd the Dean. (I lead a Heart.)
"But dearest Friends, they say, must part.
"His Time was come, he ran his Race;
"We hope he's in a better Place.

VIII Conclusion

Like John Greenleaf Whittier, Swift in his maturity had no illusions about his poetry. Whittier's comments, "I should not dare to warrant any of my work for a long drive," [34] or "I am not one of the master singers and don't pose as one," [35] might have been Swift's. His own remark was: "I have been only a Man of Rhymes, and that upon Trifles. . . ." [36] And at the end of his poem called a "Left-handed Letter to Dr. Sheridan" (1718), he added, "I beg your Pardon for using my left Hand, but I was in great Haste, and the other Hand was employed at the same Time in writing some Letters of Business." However much else is involved, the artist who takes himself too seriously or who uses his talents wrongly—as Swift did in his odes written during the Moor Park days—or who fails to take his work seriously enough does not achieve first ranking. Swift is not one of our great poets. Nevertheless, I think we need no excuse for discounting his own self-disparagement of his poetic talents; and I certainly cannot believe that we should join Samuel Johnson in such a near dismissal of his poetry, as this: "In the Poetical Works of Dr. Swift there is not much upon which the critick can exercise his powers." [37]

To answer the question, "What is poetry?" in terms that will include Swift is not my intention. The problem is obvious enough, however: one must accommodate himself to the truth that some very endearing poetic traditions find absolutely no expression in Swift's poetry. For example, the sort of exultation that Handel or Bach put into music, or that Keats put into verse, would, I sus-pect, have merely embarrassed Swift, even if his experience of and in the world had given him anything much to exult about. It had not. Furthermore, if we believe the doctrine current in some circles today, that what is stated is not literature and what is not stated is truth, then Swift is not, in his poetry, a literary figure at all. He stated. Or if we agree with T. S. Eliot that "the more per-fect the artist, the more completely separate in him will be the man who suffers and the mind which creates," [38] we will have to agree that Swift comes very far from perfection; for Swift's poems are enormously, and for the most part immediately, re-vealing statements of what was in his heart and on his mind. He was almost always in his poems, therefore.

All things considered, however, we need not apologize. At their best, Swift's poems are, like the man, bright and clever; strong, sometimes very wise, and usually very disturbing. They do occa-sionally distort reality in its difficult passage into words, but the distortion is generally in a healthy direction. That their author also had, and frequently demonstrated, "a Kind of Knack at Rhyme" [39] is merely the happiest kind of bonus.

CHAPTER 5

Cathedral Dean and Patriot

ABOUT midway through his long exile from England, Swift
wrote (March 21, 1730) that, unless he left Ireland, he would
die there "like a poisoned rat in a hole." [1] He never received the
English appointment that would allow him to leave Ireland, and
he did die in Ireland—but more a national hero than "a poisoned
rat." Nonetheless, the cheerful and confident note that marks
much of *The Journal to Stella* becomes increasingly less heard as
the years pass. "I never wake without finding life a more insignifi-
cant thing than it was the day before," he wrote in 1729.[2] Much of
his later prose is characterized by this tone, though happily by no
means the whole of it. After all, as he reported in a letter to John
Gay and the Duchess of Queensbury (July 10, 1732), his "rule" of
life was *"Vive la bagatelle!"* [3] The love of fun rarely deserted him
for long.

In a revealing comment to Pope (January 10, 1721), Swift said:
"In a few weeks after the loss of that excellent Princess [Queen
Anne], I came to my station here; where I have continued ever
since in the greatest privacy, and utter ignorance of those events
which are commonly talked of in the world. . . . I had indeed
written some Memorials of the four last years of the Queen's reign.
. . . [Also] I have written in this kingdom, a discourse to per-
suade the wretched people to wear their own manufactures instead of those from England: This Treatise soon spread very fast,
being agreeable to the sentiments of the whole nation. . . ." [4]

In this significant letter Swift not only described his drab years
following the death (1714) of Queen Anne, the fall of the Tory
party soon afterwards, and his return to Dublin; he also signaled
the beginning of an astounding time of creativity, a period that
began with *A Proposal for the Universal Use of Irish Manufacture* (1720) and continued with *A Letter to a Young Lady*

(1723), *The Drapier Letters* (1724–25), *Gulliver's Travels* (1726), *A Modest Proposal* (1729)—to mention only the most outstanding prose works, and to say nothing whatsoever about the many good poems.

I The Letter to a Young Gentleman Lately Entered into Holy Orders

The Letter to a Young Gentleman was dated January 9, 1720, and was purportedly written "By a Person of Quality." The letter, apparently not directed to or at any special person,[5] is actually a sort of vest-pocket "Handbook for all Preachers, especially Young Ones." In addition, and incidentally, it is useful as an introduction to Jonathan Swift, D.D., Dean of St. Patrick's Cathedral. In *The Letter to a Young Gentleman,* it is, as usual, important to be alert, however, to any distinction between Swift and the character he creates to do the narrating for him. In the *Tale*-volume, recognition of such a distinction does not seem to me essential; in *Gulliver's Travels,* it generally is, as it also is in this *Letter*. Furthermore, if a narrator (a persona) is used, then it is important to establish Swift's attitude toward him. These two responsibilities are easily discharged with regard to *The Letter to a Young Gentleman.*

Swift depicts his writer as a knowledgeable, very sober layperson, fairly well along in life, with many clerical friends; also this poor fellow apparently has total recall of all the bad sermons he has ever heard. He is direct and clear in what he wants to say: ". . . my Design in this Paper was not so much to instruct you in your business, either as a Clergyman, or a Preacher, as to warn you against some Mistakes. . . ." So dignified, sensible, and forthright a character Swift must have approved of and wanted us to listen to with respect.

His intention stated, our narrator begins immediately to make specific recommendations. He advises the young preacher to heed his style (style is defined as "Proper Words in proper Places"); to avoid "hard Words" (some of them, like *Attribute* and *Excentrick,* have long since passed into common use); to refrain from *reading* his sermons to the congregation; to reject the temptation to be a wit ("it is very near a Million to One, that you have none"); to check any impulse to explain, and so eliminate, the mysteries of the Christian religion ("Providence intended there should be mysteries"); and, most of all, to appeal not to the passions of his people but to their understanding and reason ("I do not see how this Talent of moving the Passions, can be of any great Use towards directing Christian men in the Conduct of their Lives").

Our Lay-Patron, as the narrator is termed on the title page of the 1720 Dublin edition, recounted an anecdote to enforce his last directive: "A Lady asked him, coming out of Church, whether it were not a very moving Discourse? Yes, said he, I was extremely sorry, for the Man is my Friend." Behind the narrator, Swift's sardonic voice is crystal clear. This same voice unremittingly for a lifetime derided and despised the "moving discourse" of Jack and all his like in *A Tale of a Tub*, or wherever it made its characteristically undisciplined appearance.

The concluding section of this *Letter* deals with "the frequent Custom of preaching against Atheism, Deism, [and] Free Thinking. . . ." The letter writer disapproves of such preaching. His premises accepted, his protests are as powerful now as they were then. For example, he says: "Reasoning will never make a Man correct an ill Opinion, which by Reasoning he never acquired." He insists that atheistical writings are a symptom of corruption in the nation, not a cause of it. He observes that a civilized state is one that includes learning and religion. The "Young Gentleman Lately entered into Holy Orders" is given, finally, this cryptic, no-nonsense decree: "the two principal Branches of Preaching, are first to tell the People what is their Duty; and then to convince them that it is so." This decree could serve then or now as an appropriate motto over the door of almost any young preacher's study.

In a different mood, Swift was capable of giving quite a different kind of counsel. In "Advice to a Parson. An Epigram" (1723), he cynically answers a question:

> Wou'd you rise in the Church, be Stupid and Dull,
> Be empty of Learning, of Insolence full:
> Tho' Lewd and Immoral, be Formal and Grave,
> In Flatt'ry an Artist, in Fawning a Slave,
> No Merit, no Science, no Virtue is wanting
> In him, that's accomplish'd in Cringing and Canting. . . .

Fortunately, Swift did not himself follow his "Advice to a Parson." It is a great deal more likely that he tried to heed his own lay-patron's advice in *The Letter to a Young Gentleman Lately entered into Holy Orders* (1720). For Swift, ordained priest in 1695, thereafter gave nearly half a century of active service to his church; and all the evidence says that he took his work as a dean and as a preacher very seriously. Hawkesworth reports the charming story of young Swift's declaration before he went to Laracor: "he hoped . . . by constant application he should so far excel that the sexton might sometimes be asked on a Sunday morning, 'Pray does the doctor preach today'?" [6] The story, if true, is not inconsistent with the fact that Swift's deepest interest in the church was more temporal than spiritual, or even doctrinal. "The state of the Church, its weaknesses, its inherited and contemporary difficulties—these," as Louis Landa quite rightly indicates, "are the matters that principally preoccupied him." [7] Evidence also suggests that, though Swift often scorned those who were concerned only with professional advancement and would go to any length to obtain it, sore annoyed was *he* without it. [8] Nonetheless, despite personal frustrations, he was a great dean; and, if not a great preacher, he was a sincere, conscientious one.

Unfortunately, most of his extant sermons read like "pamphlets"—an epithet which Mrs. Pilkington and Dr. Delany record that Swift himself applied to them. [9] Inclined to belittle his sermons, Swift once wrote to the Reverend John Winder: "Those sermons [written by Swift] You have thought fitt to transcribe will utterly disgrace You. . . . They were what I was firmly resolved to burn and especially some of them the idlest trifling stuff that ever was writt, calculated for a Church without a company or a roof. . . ." [10]

This comment must not, however, be taken literally. In any case, there is at least one lively sermon which he need never have belittled. It would keep a congregation interested and awake (and perhaps also outraged) in almost any age. This sermon begins with a cutting edge: "I have chosen these Words with Design, if possible, to disturb some Part in this Audience of half an Hour's Sleep, for the Convenience and Exercise whereof this Place, at this Season of the Day, is very much celebrated." Entitled "Upon Sleeping in Church," this sermon stands out not only as an able defense of the Cloth against unjust attack, but also as an effective indictment of behavior still existing in some churches. Swift concludes thusly this memorable discourse: "[Such] indecent Sloth is very much owing to that Luxury and Excess Men usually practice upon this Day, by which half the Service thereof is turned into Sin; Men dividing the Time between God and their Bellies, when after a gluttonous Meal, their Senses dozed and stupified, they retire to God's House to sleep out the Afternoon. Surely, Brethren, these Things ought not so to be." He was right. They ought not so to be.

To speak of Swift as a preacher is, at the end, to speak of a tantalizing gap in our knowledge.[11] There is very little contemporary comment about him as a preacher. Mrs. Pilkington, having attended a communion service at St. Patrick's, professed herself "charmed to see with what a becoming piety the dean performed that solemn service." [12] This statement does not add significantly to our sum of knowledge. Also, though Swift must have preached hundreds of sermons, only twelve have ever been printed; and one of these twelve may not be authentic. However, though we lack facts, there is no reason to assume that he strayed much from the advice he gave the "young gentleman" in *The Letter to a Young Gentleman Lately entered into Holy Orders*": "Tell the People what is their duty; . . . convince them that it is so"; avoid "hard words"; put "proper words in proper places"; appeal not to the passions, but to reason.

II A Letter to a Young Lady on her Marriage

The two most significant differences between *A Letter to a Young Lady* and *The Letter to a Young Gentleman* are (1) that Swift in *A Letter to a Young Lady* (written, 1723; first published, 1727) speaks in his own voice; and (2) that he is known to have originally directed the letter quite specifically to one person in his cathedral city of Dublin: Deborah Staunton,[13] a young woman who had recently married a man "for some Years past my particular Favourite": John Rochfort.

The fifty-six-year-old dean attempts in this letter to advise a young woman who is just settling into marriage. At first glance, it might possibly seem that the new bride to whom the letter was sent must have had distinctly mixed emotions, ones verging from gratitude to terror. The lady is told to be modest in her deportment; to "abate a little of that violent Passion for fine Cloathes"; to be careful in matters of personal cleanliness ("For the satyrical part of mankind will needs believe, that it is not impossible to be very fine and very filthy"); to improve her mind by reading; to engage in intelligent conversation "in company with Men of learning" rather than to "consult with the Woman who sits next . . . about a new Cargo of Fans."

All this advice is the good, if run-of-the-mill counsel, that a girl expects to get from her elders. We may assume that Deborah Staunton was polite enough to be grateful.[14] There are more surprising strokes. One is the wise suggestion about dress: let it be "one Degree lower than your Fortune can afford." Another is the insight, unusual coming from a man, that middle-aged women— visiting in the afternoon; playing cards at night—are very generally regarded with a particularly harsh and virulent contempt by "the younger Part of *their own Sex*" (my italics). Such counsel and such insights cause us to agree with Lord Orrery's remark: "This Letter ought to be read by all new married women, and will be read with pleasure and advantage by the most distinguished and accomplished ladies."[15] One can also at this point appreciate a more modern comment by Louis Landa: "[This] is a very charming letter welcoming to the Deanery circle a very young lady, whose parents and husband were alike Swift's particular friends."[16]

To some people, however, the letter has seemed to be a puzzling kind of "welcome" "to the Deanery circle" or to any circle at all. Must the bride be told that her parents "failed . . . in too much neglecting to cultivate [her] mind"? Must she be informed so flatly, now, that a wise man "soon grows weary of acting the Lover"? Must she be warned "against the least Degree of Fondness to [her] Husband before any Witnesses?" Must Swift "hope" that this new bride will not be such a "fool" as to "still dream of Charms and Raptures; which Marriage ever did, and ever will put a sudden end to"? What sort of a friendly letter of welcome is this!

It is just the same a friendly letter. We must understand that some of the harshest and shrewdest barbs are aimed not at Deborah Staunton but quite impersonally at "the generality of your

Sex." It is they who employ "more Thought, Memory, and Application to be Fools, than would serve to make them wise." We feel it is they, not Deborah, who would worry their husbands into buying a new equipage instead of paying the butcher's bill; it is this "Knot of Ladies, got together by themselves," to chit-chat ("about a new Cargo of Fans") rather than attend to and take part in intelligent conversation with the entire company—it is *they* who are a "very School of Impertinence and Detraction."

Furthermore, the letter is written in the straightforward terms of one reasonable person appealing to the good sense of another equally reasonable person. For the great Dean of St. Patrick's to write in such terms must have been flattering to this very young person. Finally, and of most importance, we have to meet head-on the criticism suggested previously, and neatly epitomized by so early a commentator as Mrs. Pilkington (Deborah Staunton "did not take [the *Letter*] as a compliment, either to her or the sex" [17]), and later, by Temple Scott ("There is so little reverence for the individual addressed . . . that one can hardly wonder the precepts of so stern a Mentor were received by the Lady to whom they addressed with more pique than complaisance").[18]

If this *Letter* is read aright, Mrs. Pilkington and Temple Scott are wrong. I would say that a right reading begins with the knowledge that Swift's posture is from the first sentence ironical, and that Deborah Staunton and the Rochforts were aware of this. After the personal address of "Madam," Swift wrote: "The Hurry and *Impertinence* of receiving and paying Visits on Account of your Marriage, being now over; you are beginning to enter into a Course of Life, where you will want much Advice to divert you from falling into many *Errors, Fopperies,* and *Follies to which your Sex is subject*" (my italics). *Impertinence,* so egregiously the wrong word (but so right, too), signals at once the author's ironical stance. Immediately following is the reference to the "Errors, Fopperies, and Follies to which your sex is subject." Swift had been barking at females for years. Could Deborah not have known this?

I think it is fairly obvious that Swift was playing, again, his game of tease-and-jab. In these first sentences he is teasing, and the rest of the short, first paragraph sustains this posture. He speaks of the groom ("for some years past my particular Favorite"); his long-cherished hope that Deborah might make herself "worthy of him" (!!); of the lamentable fact that her parents (old friends of his) had "failed" to "cultivate [Deborah's] mind." Finally, this great and formidable dean announced that he would be her director "as long as I shall think you deserve it, by letting you know how to act, and what you ought to avoid." I do not mean to allow the conclusion that Swift's rhetorical stance in this letter is all this sort of *bagatelle*—all tease. A fair share of jabs are there, too, as we have seen. But they are enveloped in a tone of affectionate irony that could not possibly have given offense. Deborah probably did not faint in terror when she received this letter; indeed, we do not know what she did. But I very much suspect that she laughed delightedly.

Swift liked the role of tutor to a young lady—witness his relationship with Stella and Vanessa. It is interesting to see him again play that role and do so with the healthy conviction that a young lady had to *work* at making a success of her marriage, with the characteristically bleak conviction that the young lady who marries had best forget about love, and with the teasing and kindly authority of a wise old friend.

Two phrases in the *Letter* direct us to *Gulliver's Travels*. To be sure, *"le mythe animal"* [19] is present in much of Swift's writing, but the particular application of that metaphor is directly suggestive of *Gulliver's Travels*. The relevant passage finds Swift saying that, when he reflects on the foolish behavior of females, he "cannot conceive [them] to be human Creatures, but a Sort of Species hardly a Degree above a Monkey; who hath more diverting tricks than any of [them]; is an Animal less mischievous and expensive." In another passage, Swift writes that English ladies ought to relish discourse about "Travels into remote Nations"—a clear intimation of a text to be published in three years and on which he was even now working: *Travels into several Remote Nations. . .* , by Lemuel Gulliver.

III   A Modest Proposal

A Modest Proposal is the most brilliant of a long series of Irish tracts by Swift. Ireland first learned about the *Proposal* in an advertisement in the Dublin *Intelligence* for November 8, 1729: "The late apparent spirit of patriotism, or love to our country, so abounding of late, has produced a new scheme, said in public to be written by D—— S——, wherein the author . . . ingenuously advises that one fourth part of the infants under two years old, be forthwith fattened, brought to market and sold for food, reasoning that they will be dainty bits for landlords, who as they have already devoured most of the parents, seem to have the best right to eat up the children." [20]

The character who "writes" the *Modest Proposal* is one, like Gulliver and the hack writer of the *Tale*-volume, that Swift will condemn for a moral obtuseness. The "modest" fellow who presents the *Proposal* invites our confidence (as does Gulliver), by a conversational and polite tone and by an appearance of common sense and objectivity, only to betray it (as does Gulliver also). More specifically, the narrator poses as an economic projector. As a "project," his proposal belongs to a well-defined genre popular in Swift's day. For example, just a year earlier (1728) the tireless Daniel Defoe had published his *Augusta Triumphans. Or, the Way to make London the most flourishing City in the Universe,* a publication which is a veritable portfolio of projects. It includes, among others, "A proposal to prevent murder. . . ," "A proposal to prevent the expensive importation of foreign musicians. . . ," a proposal to save "youths" and "servants" by clearing the streets of "shameless and impudent strumpets." As an *economic* projector, Swift's narrator belongs in the group of economic theorists of Swift's or any day who are either innately or perversely blind, perhaps in the name of religion or science, to the fact that people are neither animals, or things, or numbers. As Martin Price says, "the Modest Proposer is not only a typical projector but, more important, . . . [a] political arithmetician." [21]

In 1720, Swift had written to his friend John Ford: "I believe my self not guilty of too much veneration for the Irish [House of Lords], but I differ from you in Politicks[;] the Question is whether People ought to be Slaves or no." [22] Swift's unhappiness at England's unjust treatment of Ireland was by no means new in 1729, when *A Modest Proposal* appeared, or in 1720, when he made his comment to Ford. As early as 1707 his concern had found expression in his *Story of the Injured Lady.* The "Injured Lady" of this account was Ireland, and the injurer was England.

But the strongest onslaught was to begin in 1720 with *The Proposal for the Universal Use of Irish Manufacture;* it continued with the notorious *Drapier Letters* of 1724–25; it was sustained by *A Short View of Ireland* in 1727; and, though the attack did not cease in 1729, it reached its artistic culmination with the publication of *A Modest Proposal.* But it must be remembered that when Swift fought for Ireland and its people, he had most in mind the Anglo-Irish who belonged to the Established Church.[23] Anglo-Irish Presbyterians were anathema; the native Irish did not much figure in his calculations on freedom. Also, over the years, Swift's anger against the English was certainly compounded with his contempt for the Irish because of the shameful way they submitted to, in fact in some ways invited, injustice.

A good introduction to *A Modest Proposal* is Swift's *Short View of the State of Ireland,* published two years earlier in 1727. It is an uncomplicated performance, presented by a nonironic persona (somewhat like the narrator in a *Letter to a Young Gentleman*) who in about a half a dozen pages methodically presents the facts which kindled the terrible satire of the *Proposal.* According to the *Short View,* the wretched and miserable state of Ireland was due to the fact that "Ireland is the only Kingdom I ever heard or read of, either in ancient or modern Story, which was denied the Liberty of exporting their native Commodities and Manufactures. . . ."[24] Moreover, "One third Part of the Rents of Ireland, is spent in England. . . ," and "The Rise of our Rents is squeezed out of the very Blood, and Vitals, and Cloaths, and Swellings of the Tenants; who live worse than English Beggars." However, "Both sexes [in Ireland], but especially the Women, despise and abhor to wear any of their own Manufactures, even those which are better made than in other countries. . . ." We should note that Swift scolds the Irish, as well as the English; for the Irish bring misery on themselves.

Other facts were the terrible Irish famines of the preceding three years,[25] to which Swift does not refer explicitly, probably because they were on so many people's minds anyway. We learn additional "facts" from M. B. Drapier's *Letter to the Whole People of Ireland* (1724), in which Swift caused his Drapier to declare to the Irish:

. . . by the Laws of God, of NATURE, of NATIONS, and of your
Country, you ARE and OUGHT to be as FREE a People as your
Brethren in England.

The Remedy is wholly in your own Hands. . . .[26]

In view of the sort of information listed above, the narrator of
A Modest Proposal is entirely in character as a reasonable man
when he suggests that Irish babies be butchered and sold for
meat. In so terrible a situation, what else could be done? He is
also reasonable when he proposes a thrifty consequence of the
slaughter: the babies' skin "will make admirable gloves for ladies,
and summer boots for fine gentlemen." As he methodically proceeds ("There is likewise another great Advantage in my
Scheme") to tote up his sums ("of the Hundred and Twenty
Thousand Children, already computed, Twenty thousand may be
reserved for Breed"), Swift's demurrals are perfectly distinct:
"these are not advantages; this is not a modest proposal; however disagreeable the child may be, she must not be considered
merely an animal 'to be reserved for Breed'."

An arithmetic projector who believes that he has found a "fair,
cheap and easy method of making . . . children sound useful
members of the commonwealth" ought to be listened to. The situation in Ireland was so desperate that almost anybody would
get a hearing. This particular projector had the wonderful advantage of being objective, knowledgeable, and engagingly modest.
In truth, the distresssing situation in Ireland could only be cured
if people would imitate the "Modest Proposer." There is no
doubt that this man's method and his attitude towards the problem were right. "Come, let us reason together" was the appeal.
Who could resist?

The trouble was not the method or the attitude, but the monster who employed them. Blind to human misery, he was incapable of realizing that people are not animals, or things, or numbers.
He was a terrifyingly dangerous sort of person because he was so
objective, so knowledgeable, so modest, so limited, and so perfectly convinced that his conclusion was the best one thus far
proposed. He insists, "I am not so violently bent upon my own
Opinion, as to reject any offer . . . which shall be found equally

innocent, cheap, easy, and effectual." And he concludes: ". . . I have not the least personal Interest, in endeavouring to promote this necessary Work. . . . I have no Children, by which I can propose to get a single Penny; the youngest being nine Years Old and my Wife past Child-bearing."

Most immediately, *The Modest Proposal* was Swift's contribution to the human predicament in Ireland in 1729. I would agree with Edward W. Rosenheim's valuable discovery that, originally, the essay was primarily intended to voice Swift's monumental anger against the ruling class in Ireland for enduring with such spineless stupidity a situation which it was in their power to cure, and that this reading does give to *The Proposal* a unity that other readings lack.[27] But I do not think that isolating the contemporary "satiric target" necessarily explains the tremendous impact of the work today. Swift's *Proposal* is to be regarded as an unsurpassed example of sustained irony, and for that reason, if for no other, it will be remembered in our language. Much more fundamental than a recognition of the rhetoric, however, is the fact that people become angry when they read this essay. The narrator is a monster: he has no right to talk about people as "breeders"; about babies, as meat. Thus by indirection is established the thesis most relevant to today, and the main reason for its power in our times. That this reason is not the primary one Swift intended is interesting but not important. Neither did the architect intend his tower at Pisa to be remembered because it leans. Swift's *A Modest Proposal* is memorable not as an indictment of the ruling class in Ireland in 1729 but as a warning. It warns that the easy way to solve the problem of human misery is to give it to some modest-seeming, prudent-talking, thing-oriented political arithmetician and plug the ears when the screams begin.

CHAPTER 6

Gulliver's Travels

GULLIVER was probably "born" sometime early in 1714 during one of the meetings of the Scriblerus Club. The club's incredible assemblage of Tory geniuses—Pope, Parnell, Arbuthnot, Gay, and Swift were the mainstays—conceived the idea of a combined satiric project, the purpose of which Alexander Pope later described as being to ridicule "all the false tastes in learning, under the character of a man of capacity enough, that has *dipped* into every art and science, but *injudiciously* in each" [1] (my italics). Among his other activities, the central character of this project was apparently at one time intended to travel to some foreign lands; and Jonathan Swift was the one given the task of reporting on his travels.[2] Called "Martinus Scriblerus" in the Scriblerus Club project, Martinus is generally thought to be the original of the Gulliver of *Gulliver's Travels*. He is a familiar metaphor, the loyal native who travels to a remote nation (or nations) and is soon or late obliged to make a comparative evaluation of what he sees. Nobody has ever been sole proprietor of this device. For example, Plato, Lucian, and More had used it long before Swift, who was familiar with the works of all these men.[3] The device is of course still employed: one of the more recent evidences of it appears in Durrell's *Clea* (1960), in which is recorded the account of "A team of Chinese anthropologists [who] arrived in Europe to study our habits and beliefs. Within three weeks they were all dead. They died of uncontrollable laughter. . . ."

Furthermore, Swift was to employ his Gulliver as he had many of his other fictive characters: as more or less of a mask, behind or through which he would speak. I say "more or less of a mask" because sometimes the mask slips away, as in Book III of the *Travels*, and he speaks quite directly to us. But, as a rule, the rhetorical posture in the *Travels* is ironical and therefore Swift's voice—or voices, for sometimes he is saying several things—is different from Gulliver's.

As early as 1711 Swift had created a character somewhat suggestive of Gulliver. The character is a traveler by the name of Sieur du Baudrier, who, as servant to Matthew Prior, pretended to report on the latter's negotiations to end the War of the Spanish Succession. The Sieur du Baudrier's sober and "factual" account, purportedly "translated" into English, effectively served Swift's and the Tory party's intention of putting a favorable front on Prior's visit.[4] The Sieur du Baudrier is dull as a character; but he is at least interesting as an early example of Swift's use of this sort of mask. However, exactly where Swift got his idea and precisely when he first settled in his mind on the attributes of the character that eventually became Gulliver are questions that probably will never be settled to everybody's satisfaction. In any event, the questions are not of essential critical import. Besides, they can be settled only on the basis of facts, and these are lacking.

Happily, in Swift's letters to John Ford facts are available about the dates and the chronology involved in the composition of the *Travels*. Though these letters do not tell when he began the actual writing of his great book, they do indicate that he was busy writing it in 1721; that, before the close of 1723, he had completed his account of Gulliver's first two voyages; that he finished the fourth voyage by January, 1724; that he then began the third voyage but, because of the interruption caused by his writing of *The Drapier Letters*, did not finish it until the middle of 1725.[5] *Gulliver's Travels* was published in 1726 and, thanks to Alexander Pope's "prudent management" of the book's printing, it can be said that Swift's greatest book made him some money. Otherwise, he said, "I never got a farthing by anything I writ, . . ." [6]

I *Reactions to* Gulliver's *"Sting"*

Gulliver's Travels meets two simple working definitions of a classic: it speaks powerfully and significantly to each generation; it never yields it full meaning. Any rereading is a new experience. In a sense, a rereading is in fact impossible since every thoughtful reading brings revelations that turn the book into a different one than it was before.

For some readers, *Gulliver's Travels* lacks one attribute, possibly not essential to, but at any rate possessed by, some of our greatest books: it is too negative; it offers no solution to the problem which it defines. Thus, if the book is taken as a revelation of the evil that in us lies, it gives no vision that encompasses evil and, without palliating it, makes it at least for a moment bearable and perhaps somehow even understandable. Yet, despite this one reservation, testimony is well-nigh universal that *Gulliver's Travels* is one of the great books of the world.

Swift's most famous comment about his greatest book is the one he wrote to Pope in 1725: ". . . the chief end I propose to my self in all my labors is to vex the world rather than divert it." [7] He was distressed when Benjamin Motte, the London publisher, made some unauthorized changes in the 1726 (first) edition. These alterations were corrected in the 1735 Faulkner edition, but meanwhile Swift had complained dourly to Ford, ". . . the whole Sting is taken out in several passages, in order to soften them. Thus the Style is debased, the humor quite lost, and the matter insipid." [8] The readers of Swift's day did not agree that "the humor [was] quite lost, and the matter insipid." Nor were they noticeably vexed. The reaction of his friends is typified by a letter from John Arbuthnot: "Gulliver is a happy man that at his age can write such a merry work." [9] John Gay wrote a letter which indicates what an immediate and overwhelming success the book was with the general reading public: "About ten days ago a book was published here of the travels of one Gulliver, which has been the conversation of the whole town ever since: the whole impression sold in a week. . . . From the highest to the lowest it is universally read, from the Cabinet-council to the Nursery." [10]

The popular acclaim which Gay referred to is typical of the response accorded *Gulliver's Travels* in the early years of its publication. Although the interesting history of critical reaction thereafter is not properly the subject of this book,[11] we may note briefly, however, that the merry enthusiasm of most of Gulliver's first readers did not last very long. Samuel Johnson, in his *Life of Swift* (1781), gives a fair summation of middle and late eighteenth-century opinion: "Criticism [of *Gulliver's Travels*] was for a while lost in wonder: . . . But when distinctions came to be made the part which gave least pleasure was that which describes the Flying Islands, and that which gave most disgust must be the history of the Houyhnhnms." [12] During the nineteenth-century, criticism was generally condemnatory. It is perhaps not too much to say that nineteenth-century critics felt Swift's "sting" and resented it—sometimes hysterically. For example, in his *English Humourists of the Eighteenth Century* (published 1853), William Thackeray looked upon the moral of *Gulliver's Travels* and thought it "horrible, shameful, unmanly, blasphemous." [13] Leslie Stephen felt that Book IV was a "ghastly caricature," "lamentable and painful." [14]

Modern criticism is calmer, unsentimental, and probable better informed than anything that precedes. One reason is that in our day an impressive amount of research has revealed so much about the mind and art and times of Mr. Swift; also, modern criticism has been most helpfully perceptive, particularly with respect to Books III and IV. Finally, and doubtless also a factor, this new appreciation of Swift has been helped because the events of this century have conditioned readers to accept more readily Swift's austere and gloomy vision. The critical history of *Gulliver's Travels* therefore indicates that Swift was just about right in his own remark: "The world glutted it self with that book at first, and now it will go off but soberly, but I suppose will not be soon worn out." [15]

II *Various Ways of Reading the Book*

There are many ways to read *Gulliver's Travels*. A few ways, here referred to in general terms, will be explored later in more detail. First, then, *Gulliver's Travels* is a satire on travel books and on those, like Gulliver, who write them—or show them in our day on slides. Such people do not always sort out the trivial from the important experience: they show and tell everything. *Gulliver's Travels* is a story, too, often a very funny one (though it is not a novel). It is also topical satire on people and events of the day. It is allegory, and, as such, it is an indictment of man for his pride, for his abuse of his fellows, for his dirtiness, and for his perverse refusal to look long enough and accurately enough at the surface of things so that, seeing beneath, he may learn the difference between the shell and the kernel, between truth and falsehood, between good and evil.

In addition, because an author inevitably informs his work with his own mind and personality, *Gulliver's Travels* can be read in part and incidentally as a depiction of Swift himself. Probably some readers do read the book primarily in this fashion; but this approach, legitimate for autobiography, limits a great imaginative prose satire. Finally, in our times, the Gulliver who comes home from his fourth voyage might even be regarded as a dedicated but third-rate artist-figure who is almost completely alienated from the society around him. Though I think some of these ways are better than others, what it comes to is that the more reasonably intelligent ways men and women read *Gulliver's Travels,* the more pleasure they will get from it.

III   *A Voyage to Lilliput*

The first impression this book creates on the reader is probably that of verisimilitude. Facing the beginning of the first chapter is a map, and it looks accurate and real; but it is in fact neither. Swift begins in the same fashion each of the accounts of Gulliver's four voyages; it is one of the many recurring devices in his book. He also includes pictorial representations of various sorts; and, as a letter to his publisher reveals, he thought them important[16] because they undeniably gave the appearance of truth-telling to his account.

The early pages of *Gulliver's Travels* demand an unusually attentive reading. For example, on the very first page are those carefully chosen details that suggest accurate and honest reporting. Gulliver spent "three years" at "Emanuel-College in Cambridge"; he "studied Physick" at Leyden for "two years and seven Months"; he "married Mrs. Mary Burton, second Daughter to Mr. Edmund Burton." These and other details dispose us to suspend immediately any possibility of disbelief about this obviously true voyage of this undoubtedly honest "man" who is about to take a trip to Lilliput.

The first sentence of this first page reads, "My Father had a small estate in Nottinghamshire; I was the third of five sons." The "I" is Gulliver, the narrator of these travels. He is the "mask" behind and through which Swift speaks. It is, as usual, important to realize immediately something of what this narrator—Lemuel Gulliver—is, and is not. The "small estate" in Nottinghamshire makes him a member of the *middle* class living in the *middle* of

England. As "the third of five sons" he is clearly the *middle* son. Though the repetition was probably not intentional and certainly proves nothing, it may be taken as suggestive: Gulliver is a middling sort of person, a sort of Mr. Average.[17]

As with some of his poetry, the first page of Swift's *Gulliver's Travels* raises again the problem of scatology. One way to face this problem is to ignore it; a second way is to expurgate all offensive passages from the texts that young people will read. (But this seldom works very well since the expurgators, though they have mean and vulgar minds, seldom have really dirty minds. A few lewd passages inevitably escape them.) A third way is to leave offensive passages in the book but to be embarrassed by them. A fourth way is that of those psychoanalysts who have found Swift's writings a rich and irresistible vein to explore. *The Psychoanalytic Review* of 1942 offers an instance of this approach. As there explained, *Gulliver's Travels* presents "abundant evidence of the neurotic makeup of the author and discloses in him a number of perverse trends indicative of fixation at the anal sadistic state of libidinal development. Most conspicuous among those perverse trends is that of coprophilia, although the work furnishes evidence of numerous other related neurotic characteristics accompanying the general picture of psychosexual infantilism and emotional immaturity." [18]

It is just not true to insinuate, as these remarks seem to, that Swift passed all his time fluttering dirtily in and around the bathroom. His so-called scatology can be quite adequately explained in terms of his era and of its literary traditions, to which Swift was always sensitive. Thus Irvin Ehrenpreis concludes, in probably the most enlightened chapter yet written on Swift's "obscenity": "Swift's writing is sometimes coarse or bawdy. . . . If we are shocked, let us admit it is traditions that shock us, not the man." [19] Swift said about his poems that he wrote "never any without a moral View," [20] and I think he would like us to believe that all his major prose works merit the same comment. But this moral intention does not exclude his obvious desire sometimes simply to have fun with filth. That is all he is doing with his word play on the first page of *Gulliver's Travels*, when he sports coyly with *Mr. James Bates*. James Bates becomes successively *Mr. Bates;* then *my good master, Mr. Bates; Mr. Bates, my master;* and finally at the bottom of the page,[21] since there was not much sense in teetering on the edge of this sorry joke much longer, *my good master Bates*. An ancient tradition, including such figures in the history of English literature as Chaucer and Shakespeare, would certainly permit Swift to have this sort of harmless fun and even, on occasion, actually to enjoy "the jolly coarseness of life." [22]

Very early in Book I a major recurring device appears that helps to unify both structurally and thematically, the whole of the *Travels*. This device is the accident which precipitates Gulliver into the central action of each book. In Book I it is a shipwreck. Actually, nobody could be very much blamed for this first accident. But, by Book IV, the event which puts Gulliver in Houyhnhnmland is a betrayal by his own shipmates. Here there is blame. Thus Arthur Case's remark: "The accidents by which Gulliver arrives in the several countries which he visits are varied not only for the sake of novelty, but to keep pace with his growing realization of the defects of human nature." [23] The reader does well to look for this and other devices that give structural and thematic unity to the book.

The early pages of Book I present the little people (the six-inch tall Lilliputians) and the "little language" that appears throughout the *Travels*. These little people of Book I reveal themselves to be as small morally as they are physically. The revelation of their pettiness comes gradually to the reader, but the moment of realization must no doubt vary from reader to reader, depending on such factors as his alertness, his temperament, and his experience with irony. The timing of the moment is unimportant, just so long as he discovers somewhere along the line that his hosts on his voyage are more than merely engaging and cuddly. His hosts gossip meanly about each other; they fight over such trivial matters as which end of an egg should be broken first; and their king is angry when Gulliver refuses to help him bring a neighboring country into slavery.

About the language of these pygmies, and of the residents of other lands that Gulliver visits, critics have exercised considerable ingenuity. The attempts at translation made thus far do not seem to me to enrich markedly our reading of this text. In Book IV, the language is clearly intended to sound like the talk of horses, if horses talked. Moreover, the words of the "little language" are ob-

viously a verisimilar device, and they do occasionally have special meanings: *Gulliver* is gullible; *Tribnia* and *Langden* are
anagrams for "Britain" and "England"; *hurgo* is perhaps a rogue.
But beyond that, most of the words and names must be read as
the untranslatable language of some never-never land. Further
exploration of the problem now almost invites Mark Twain's
words: "the researches of many commentators have already
thrown much darkness on this subject, and it is probable that, if
they continue, we shall soon know nothing at all about it."

Also, early in the account of Gulliver's first voyage, we en-
counter one of the several instances in the *Travels* of satire on
travel books and travelers, probably a vestige of Swift's association
with the Scriblerus Club. The first such instance occurs in Chapter
2 when Gulliver "for some hours extremely pressed by the ne-
cessities of nature . . . was under great difficulties between ur-
gency and shame. The best expedient I could think on," he wrote,
"was to creep into my house, which I accordingly did; and shut-
ting the gate after me, I went as far as the length of my Chain
would suffer; and discharged my body of that uneasy load. . . .
I cannot but hope the candid Reader will [not be offended], after
he hath impartially considered my case, and the distress I was in."
The scatological problem, discussed above, need not interfere
with an understanding of what Swift, through Gulliver, is here
mainly protesting: the ridiculous traveler who reports everything
about his trip, even details about his bowel movements.

Finally, readers of the beginning pages of this book should be
aware of what is called its "topical" satire. For instance, when
Flimnap in Book I maintains himself in office by doing tricks on a
tightrope, Swift is satirizing a lively "topic" of the day: the political activities of Robert Walpole, the Whig Prime Minister of England. When the curious Lilliputian throngs are ordered "not to
come within fifty yards of [Gulliver's] house, without licence
from the court, whereby *the secretaries of state got considerable
fees*" (my italics), Swift is satirizing the bureaucratic thievery
usually presumed to be more or less in the nature of things in London or in Dublin. Much later, in Book III, when Laputa fails to
bring Balnibarbi to subjection, Swift is referring to Ireland's successful resistance to the introduction of Wood's copper halfpence.

But this topical aspect of *Gulliver's Travels* is customarily of little interest to a modern reader. In general, the book is read today not because it was appropriate and relevant to men and events in Swift's time, but because it meaningfully relates to men and events in our time. In the instances referred to above, therefore, the lesson for us is that oppression of any sort should be resisted, that an entrenched officialdom will inevitably exact bribes whenever possible, and that a people's leader should not win and maintain his position by spectacularly demonstrating skills which are irrelevant to what is needed. Great gymnastic skills are surely not the right criteria by which to measure a country's leader.

Now, assuming that we have read not only these early pages but the whole of Book I, what major points stand out? First, we have learned to know and like the narrator. Gulliver is for the most part an honest reporter; he is well intentioned and is very good at learning a new language. To be sure, he has now and then a startling way of not paying any regard to a crucial fact. For example, when he soberly assures us that not a particle of scandal should be attached to the relationship between him and the wife of the Lord Treasurer, his elaborate defense skirts mention of the really significant consideration: he is six feet tall and she is six inches tall. Gulliver is a trifle naïve.

Also, we know our narrator better if we are alert to the voices of irony in this unfolding narrative. In fact, as suggested above, a great part of our enjoyment comes from being on the lookout for, and discovering, these differing voices. In the reference just made to Gulliver's attempt to vindicate the reputation of a lady unjustly charged with immoral behavior, the surface meaning is of course Gulliver's. Swift's voice should also be heard, chuckling and saying something like "Isn't Gulliver silly?" The same "other" voice is noted when Gulliver urinates all over the apartment of her Imperial Majesty. He did flood the fire out, but he is perplexed when the Empress conceived "the greatest abhorrence of what I had done" and "removed to the most distant side of the court." Why should the Empress be offended? Gulliver does not understand. Again, when the Emperor announces his "lenient" decision to blind Gulliver and then starve him to death, Gulliver is distressed. He concludes that the lowness of his birth and the deficiencies in his education prevent him from regarding the sentence as lenient. Swift's voice emerges clearly: "One need have neither high birth nor extensive education to see so obvious a fact. One need only see a thing as it is. The 'thing' in this instance is cruel, not lenient." In such passages, Swift is judging Gulliver. He is not yet unrelentingly condemning, as he will be before he finishes with him; but he was already begun to insist that the words of this British sailor should be weighed. Like most people, Gulliver can't see straight sometimes; sometimes he does not see at all.

Finally, if a major thesis sustained by Book I is that Gulliver has the limitations that any average person has, an even more important assertion is that Gulliver is morally superior to the little people, his hosts. He does not have their meanness or pettiness. Therefore, measured by the moral norm that they provide, he, like any average man, has cause to be reasonably satisfied with himself. Also, like any average man who is satisfied with himself, his travels have thus far taught him nothing.

IV A Voyage to Brobdingnag

In Book II recur such structural or thematic devices as the map, the shipwreck that precipitates Gulliver into the central action of this voyage, and the usual attention given to specific detail. For example, Gulliver's first experience in this new land is to see, from a distance, a giant; then he comes upon grass twenty feet high, and corn forty feet high. Such verisimilar details speedily transport us to the usual paradox: belief in a never-never land that is.

Gulliver, just recently big in a land of little people, is now little in a land of giants. It is perhaps too much to say that a reader is thus prepared to expect that Gulliver will not fare very well, judged by the moral norms of big people. But that in fact is what happens. When the judgment is made, it appears that his is a race of "little odious vermin." Nonetheless, Gulliver yet has saving graces. He is still a fascinating reporter; he has a wonderful loyalty to his country; he is resourceful; he is well intentioned. Sometimes he again appears somewhat ridiculous: he has to swim for his life when thrown into a pitcher of cream; he rows in his large boat, which would hold eight humans (But "when I had done . . . Glumdalclitch hung it on a nail to dry"); he takes a flying leap that lands him in the middle of cow dung; to play a jig on his host's spinnit, he runs up and down a sixty-foot platform, banging away at the keys ("the most violent exercise I ever underwent").

But these activities do not seriously diminish our affection for Gulliver; instead, they illustrate once again the fact that *Gulliver's Travels* has in it a great deal of quite uncomplicated fun.

A more sober reaction to Book II develops when, on the one hand, we study what Gulliver observes and says about the Brobdingnagians and, on the other, when we hear his chief host, the Brobdingnagian king, calmly and objectively add up the meaning of all the facts that the little visitor has given him about "civilized" life in England. A major structural device of the *Travels* is the confrontation one: in each of the four books, Gulliver confronts a culture different from his own. Implicit in this confrontation is the expectation that, looking over the evidence of what he has seen, he will make an honest comparison. Montaigne does the same when he compares the culture of the Brazilian cannibals and that of Europe. In an incredibly objective study Montaigne concludes that the culture of the cannibals is in most respects distinctly superior to that of "civilized" Europe. Gulliver is not yet ready in Book II to make this type of distinction between what he confronts abroad and what he sees at home.

Three or four instances illustrate the workings of the confrontation device in Book II. In the first of these, Gulliver is on a shopping trip with his little nursemaid and friend, Glumdalclitch (She is only forty feet high). Beggars crowd around the coach he is in. He sees a woman with a cancerous breast, "full of holes, in two or three of which I could have easily crept." This sight was bad enough, but what most distressed him was the lice on these people. He could see "their snouts with which they rooted like swine." Swift's implication is all too clear: Whatever Gulliver (Man) can see on and in the skin of a giant Brobdingnagian, microscopic eyes can see on Gulliver. It is a vulgar and humbling notion: lice, "rooting like swine," are in the folds of fat in every man's belly—but not yet, for he does not see them, in Gulliver's.

In one memorable passage in Book II, Gulliver, like the narrator in "A Beautiful young Nymph going to Bed," becomes the envy of all our crowd of Peeping Toms. Gulliver is brought right into the apartments of the maids of honor, where, of course, he is still the invisible peeper; for the young ladies regard him not as a man but as a kind of toy. He watches them dress and undress.

They do not hesitate in his presence "to discharge what they had drunk, to the quantity of at least two hogs heads." (As women, incidentally, these young ladies are also invisible to Gulliver.) Seeing only the physical grossness of the body and of bodily functions, he is filled with emotions of "horror and disgust." The voice of Swift, behind Gulliver, is again saying: "Look at yourself, especially if you are a girl, and most especially if you think yourself lovely; excepting for your size, in what way are you less vulgar than these Brobdingnagians?"

One interesting feature of this boudoir scene is that the redoubtable little Gulliver faints for the first time. He could endure being placed upon the bare bosom of one of these maids of honor, for the natural smell of sixty feet of Brobdingnagian female was bearable, he discovered, though not pleasant. However, if the maid was perfumed, Gulliver "immediately swooned away." That a gigantic physical stimulus (the stench of a perfumed Brobdingnagian) should cause Gulliver to faint is entirely reasonable. Moreover, if and when Gulliver learns the major lesson of his voyages—when he learns to assess and evaluate experience—he will react consistently, intelligently, and just as emphatically to what Swift would regard as of more importance: a *moral* "smell" will cause him to faint.

But Gulliver's moral sensitivity is at this point elementary. The moral heights to which his hosts in Book II reach simply baffle him, a fact clearly demonstrated when our ingenuous little traveler gives his host an "exact account of the government of England": and his Majesty in Brobdingnagia draws a line under the evidence and states the obvious conclusion: "My little friend Grildrig, you have made a most admirable panegyric upon your country. You have clearly proved that ignorance, idleness, and vice, are the proper ingredients for qualifying a legislator. That laws are best explained, interpreted, and applied by those whose interests and abilities lie in perverting, confounding, and eluding them. I observe among you some lines of an institution, which in its original might have been tolerable; but these half erased, and the rest wholly blurred and blotted by corruptions. . . ." Therefore, by "what I [the Brogdingnagian king] have gathered from your own relation, and the answers I have with much pains wringed and extorted from you, I cannot but conclude the bulk of your natives to be the most pernicious race of little odious vermin that nature ever suffered to crawl upon the surface of the earth."

On the evidence that Gulliver gives, the indictment is as accurate as it is severe. To Gulliver at this state, however, the indictment is merely an astonishing error. With a lovely condecension he explains his host's error: the king has lived "secluded from the rest of the world" and has therefore been victimized by obvious "prejudices" and "a certain narrowness of thinking." As a consequence, Gulliver believes that, by performing what *he* considers a kind and generous act, the king will be forced to adopt a less severe and a more accurate opinion of mankind: he therefore generously offers the king the secret of gunpowder, explaining that with this weapon its owner can divide hundreds of enemy bodies in the middle, rip up pavements, dash out brains, and so on. The king is horrified at such "inhuman ideas." Gulliver's own moral blindness prevents him from any reaction other than honest bewilderment. He cannot understand why anybody should "let slip" so grand an opportunity.

So, Book II really ends with a series of questions. Gulliver has now confronted three civilizations: his own (and, roughly speaking, ours); the Lilliputians'; the Brogdingnagians'. Does he compare, evaluate, or assess? He has looked at a vision of Utopia in the "original" institutions of the Lilliputians (Chapter 6); he has seen a kind of Utopia among the large-souled Brobdingnagians. Compared, morally, with these "people," he clearly does not—and thus we do not, as Mr. Average—get off unscathed. But does Gulliver begin to think less of his own civilization or of himself? Does Gulliver think at all? Not much; not yet—but when he returns to civilization, he experiences some problems of physical maladjustment; for everything looks small to him: "I began to think myself in Lilliput. I was afraid of trampling on every traveller I met, and often called aloud to have them stand out of the way. . . . When I came to my own house, . . . one of the servants opening the door, I bent down to go in (like a goose under a gate) for fear of striking my head. My wife ran out to embrace me, but I stooped lower than her knees. [She looked so small.]" Though there are problems of physical maladjustment, there is as yet no sign in Gulliver of moral adjustment. He has no real problems yet. They will come later.

V   A *Voyage to Laputa, Balnibarbi, Glubbdubdrib, Luggnagg, and Japan*

As the letters to Ford reveal, Swift finished his "Voyage to the Houyhnhnms" (Book IV of *Gulliver's Travels*) and then commenced work on the "Voyage to Laputa, Balnibarbi, Luggnagg, Glubdubdrib, and Japan" (Book III). This accident of composition has led George Sherburn to state: "These letters [to Ford] also make it apparent that the third voyage was the last to be written. The fourth, then, should be only hesitantly regarded as the final drawing of the curtain of gloom." [24] Although this comment is astute and relevant to a biography of Swift, what is important to us is that Swift placed the "Voyage to the Houyhnhnms" last. Inasmuch as a great book must state its own theme—largely irrespective of outside biographical, philosophical, sociological, historical, psycholanalytical, bionomical, or econometrical data, however exciting and enriching the data from these sources may be—what we have to do is look at the book as it is. Book III must be studied, therefore, as Book III because that's what it is. Book IV must be regarded as Book IV and as "the final drawing of the curtain of gloom."

Book III is not generally so highly regarded as other sections of the *Travels*. The reasons are as obvious as, it seems to me, sufficient—though I should like, before finishing this discussion, to make a claim for the positive merit which this book has, and which distinguished scholars of our day have most persuasively pointed out. "[T]he part which gave the least pleasure," wrote Samuel Johnson, "is that which describes the Flying Island. . . ." [25] The story line of Book III, which includes the account of Gulliver's visit to the flying island of Laputa, is still thought to be the weakest of the entire book. It is. The construction, almost entirely episodic, consists of a series of anecdotes which develop only slight momentary suspense, as in the account of the attempt to put down the rebellion in Lindalino. Little narrative tension is anywhere long sustained. In addition, as with the *Tale*-volume, the satire seems at times rather more sprayed than aimed. To be sure, there are some specific targets. Swift's continuing interest in history and in historiography explains one of these targets: those "prostitute writers" who do not report truly "The springs and motives of great enterprises and revolutions in the world, and of the contemptible accidents to which they owed their success."

Another specific target is the idea of immortality, as it is sentimentally and naïvely understood by Gulliver. In his references to the Strulbrugs (Chapter 10) Swift insists that, since the forces of nature inexorably bring decay, it is better to die before these forces condemn the body to an old age that merely grows increasingly disgusting and horrible. The account implies gratitude that natural infirmities, which every second cause us to rot and wither away, are allowed no more time than they already have. It is reason for thanksgiving that death normally wins the race against rot.

A third specific target illustrates some of the topical satire in this book. Like *The Drapier Letters*, this section (Chapter 3) satirizes the British attempt to introduce Wood's halfpence into Lindalino (Dublin). In a half dozen paragraphs, regarded by eighteenth-century publishers as too dangerous to print, but included in modern editions, Swift recorded the failure of the British "to reduce this proud people." Though this and other specific targets may be easily enough pointed out, Book III does nonetheless lack the unity, as prose satire, of Books I, II, and IV.[26] What readers will find in this book is a Swiftean congregation of grievances, with—as we shall suggest in a moment—one offense standing out above the rest. For most readers, in other words, Book III has perhaps a dominant, rather than a unifying, theme.

Lastly, an obvious failure of Book III is Swift's unsuccessful manipulation of his narrator, Gulliver. In these four voyages, an overwhelming question continues to be; Will it ever occur to Gulliver, in his confrontation of the various cultures which he meets, to assess his own culture and himself in the light of that culture? Perhaps the revelation of damaging fact after fact may not affect Gulliver at all and he will remain unchanged by his experiences; perhaps the whole of the truth may strike him in a sudden terribly illuminating moment and the course of his life will be radically altered; or part of the truth may strike him (as it does, in Book IV) and change his life in a less desirable but no less dramatic way than if he had seen all of the truth. In Book III Swift never settled on any of these alternatives. Though Swift's own attitude is clear, we do not always know what Gulliver's reaction is.

The reason is that, though Swift now and again makes an awkward shift to remind us that it is Gulliver who is relating this account ("I [Gulliver] hope the reader need not be told that I do not in the least intend my own country in what I say upon this occasion" [chap. 6]), we do not believe him. In fact, we do not even think Gulliver is there. When we hear "I told [the host] that in the Kingdom of Tribnia [i.e., Britain] . . . the bulk of the people consisted wholly of discoverers, witnesses, informers, accusers, prosecutors, evidences, swearers. . . ," the "I" is not Gulliver at all; it is the angry voice of the panoplied Tory Dean, Jonathan Swift himself.

Swift's mismanagement of Gulliver in Book III has occasioned many interesting comments. For example, Kathleen Williams writes that, "whether or not Swift planned it so, Gulliver's virtual lack of function, indeed of existence, in the 'Voyage to Laputa' has a certain effectiveness in contributing to the atmosphere of meaningless activity and self-deceit, leading to a shadowy despair." [27] But I think even more interesting are possibilities of speculation about the *end* of Book III. The fact of a recurring pattern of return in the other three voyages sets up a certain expectation; and, since these expectations are not fulfilled, the situation does most especially invite comment.

Instead of the quite detailed accounts in the other three voyages, Gulliver's return in Book III is disposed of quite summarily. Specifically, in each of the other three voyages, Gulliver and the captain of the ship which brings him home, talk at some length. A study of the meetings between Gulliver and these captains suggests that the captain's function in each instance is to assist Gulliver in his readjustment to normal humanity—in his return, so to say, to reality. At the end of Book III, however, the captain is barely mentioned. He has almost no conversation with Gulliver. Indeed, to secure passage aboard ship, Gulliver has rejected his identity and posed as a Dutchman. Therefore, since in a sense he no longer exists, there can be no conversation between him and the captain. Perhaps this is also the reason why Gulliver has no problems of readjustment, physical or moral, at the end of the third voyage. The "real" Gulliver did not take the trip. This fact, in turn, intriguingly delivers to us the familiar mythic figure who loses his life, only to find it. The Gulliver, who ceases to exist in

Book III, is the Gulliver who is born anew in Book IV. A fetching irony and a pregnant concept to explore, it perhaps stretches ingenuity beyond allowable limits. So we will leave it.

No critic has yet proclaimed Book III to be the best work Swift ever produced. On the whole, it must still be considered a kind of satiric grab bag, with little narrative interest. But scholars and critics in our day, giving long-neglected Book III a long look, have been so illuminating in their researches and comments that it merits begin to show forth more clearly and to better effect than ever before.[28] First, a more sympathetic reading of Book III was made possible when one important misconception was removed: research proved that Swift, though he had no affection for it, was not ignorant of science; [29] he read the proceedings of the Royal Academy of Science. Also, he and his Scriblerus Club friends had apparently some notion of the fact, long before *Gulliver's Travels* was written, that the problem was not science (or art) as such, but rather the superficial dilettante who "dipped into every art and science" and "injudiciously in each." [30] If Swift sometimes erred (as he did) in his judgment of what the scientists were doing, his errors are understandable. Who could have foreseen that the sun (Vitamin C) could indeed be extracted from cucumbers? [31] Who could have foreseen that, for the twentieth-century traveler in outer space, the disposition of human excrement would present a problem requiring careful study?

Second, Book III is given some moments of great power by its one most dominent theme, one that is illustrated when Gulliver writes about his hosts' need for flappers. The Laputan, so wonderfully adept at abstract thought, must be attended by someone "employed diligently to attend his master in his walks, and upon occasion to give him a soft flap on his eyes, because he is always so wrapped up in cogitation, that he is in manifest danger of falling down every precipice, and bouncing his head against every post, and in the streets, of jostling others, or being jostled himself into the kennel." Though to get an island to fly, as these Laputans did, is a feat of astounding theoretical and practical skill, it is a skill which Swift ignored. What did impress him was that, in all matters which as a satirist he chose to observe, these abstract theorists lack the most ordinary kind of common sense. They are funny, as a result; but they are more than merely amusing. We do hear Swift laughing sardonically as Gulliver soberly reports his hosts' interest in such absurd projects as "softening marbles for pillows" and breeding "naked sheep." The laugh continues, somewhat more bitterly, when Gulliver records that, among these people, "a man born blind . . . was to mix colors." The results of such activity were patently disastrous to Gulliver's hosts and, by implication, will be equally so to any people comparably victimized at any time. This satire on what seemed to Swift the senseless and obviously impractical abstractions of projectors and pseudoscientists seems to me the one most dominant theme of Book III.

Bonamy Dobrée has a very good comment about this satire. He writes: "Swift objected to the absurd pretensions of the second-rate scientists to explain the inexplicable; he objected to the self-glorification of the petty virtuoso dissecting flies." None of these activities were of any importance. Dobrée continues: "[Swift] was really asking the question, 'What is the proper object of man's most strenuous intellectual attention?' " [32] The question needed asking in 1726; it needs asking now. That Book III, despite its obvious limitations, forces this question into prominence is the best explanation of its worth.

VI A Voyage to the Country of the Houyhnhnms

Before the disastrous fourth voyage began, Gulliver was obviously still pretty much the average man, doing and thinking as average men generally do. On his way to his ship, he left a pregnant wife behind him, just as many another sailor has through the ages. (The issue of that pregnancy was fated to accommodate itself to one of the oddest fathers in all literary history!) At any rate, Gulliver on this voyage is very speedily thrust into the central action with which Book IV is primarily concerned. His predicament this time is caused by the very worst sort of treachery: his own men betray him. Thus, as Arthur Case has said, "The accidents by which Gulliver arrives in the several countries . . . are varied . . . to keep pace with his growing realization of the defects of human nature." [33] In fact, Gulliver is not quite ready to admit to these "defects," but the realization is now certainly very near.

The action of Book IV concerns Gulliver's life with the horses (Houyhnhnms) and the revolting, monkeylike figures (Yahoos).

During his three years in the land ruled by these Houyhnhnms, Gulliver is so favorably impressed that he wishes to live out his days among them. His wish reflects the fact that he has finally "awakened." He now compares; he assesses. The result is a rejection of his own species and the civilization it has constructed. A major tension of the entire four books is thus resolved; but it is resolved very dramatically in terms which belong to the Houyhnhnm-Yahoo world.

The question is of course, "Is Gulliver a Yahoo?" If he is a Yahoo, then the species of which he is a fair representative is also Yahoo and its culture is Yahoo. Gulliver knows he is not, protests that he is not, but is finally relentlessly driven to the fact that he *is* a Yahoo. The climactic scene comes about when he gets permission from the sorrel nag—she plays the guardian role in this Book IV that Glumdalclitch plays in Book II—to wash in a river. As he stripped himself naked and bathed, he was observed by a young female Yahoo. The stripped Gulliver so teased the desires of this young female that, inflamed with passion, she assaulted our hero. "I roared as loud as I could," reported Gulliver. The sorrel nag, galloping up, saves him from what novelists used to call "a fate worse than death." Gulliver's reaction to his near-escape is a sobering one: ". . . now I could no longer deny that I was a real Yahoo in every limb and feature, since the females had a natural propensity to me, as one of their own species." Most of Book IV is concerned with validating this equation: Gulliver = Yahoo. Our task is not at this point to assess the truth of the equation; instead, it is to see how Swift "proves" his proposition. Particularly effective in this proof is the recurring device of the conversation between the traveler and his host. In this confrontation, Gulliver speaks of war ("a soldier is a Yahoo hired to kill in cold blood as many of his own species, who have never offended him, as possibly he can"). Gulliver tells about lawyers "among us," whose purpose is to prove that "white is black and black is white." He tells about doctors and how they kill off "husbands and wives grown weary of their mates." He speaks of the nobility, "bred from childhood in idleness and luxury." Now as a matter of fact, Swift numbered among his friends good and great men who were, for example, doctors (Arbuthnot was one) or nobles (even while he was writing his *Travels* his Noble friend Baron Carteret was Lord

Lieutenant of Ireland). It is clear, therefore, that Gulliver's report to his host exhibits the familiar distortion device.

Just as in important parts of all books of the *Travels,* just as in many parts of the *Tale*-volume (1704 and 1710) and in such poems as "A Beautiful Young Nymph Going to Bed" (1730), Swift's technique can be explained, though this explanation does not for a moment—at least for most readers—palliate its corrosive force. The technique is the result of a dour vision which instinctively and with such sureness searches out the most significant fact or facts (ignoring all others) in any situation and then perhaps even exaggerates these facts. As an instance we think of the Brobdingnagian nurse about whom we are given *only one distinguishing physical feature:* her "monstrous breast, [whose] nipple was about half the bigness of my head, and the hue both of that and the dug so varified with spots, pimples and freckles, that nothing could appear more nauseous" (Book II, Chapter 1). This sort of caricature of the truth is perhaps what lies behind Hugo Reichard's very shrewd observation that "[Gulliver] provides unending as well as unflattering answers to simple questions of information. . . . He is certainly a beguiling figure. It is a question whether any other double-dealer ever went undetected half so long." [34]

Swift's limited vision results in "a stacking of the cards" to incline the argument in his favor. Thus at the end of Book IV, as at the end of Book II, when the host draws a line under the evidence that Swift had allowed Gulliver to reveal, his statement of what the sum comes to is inevitably and crashingly unflattering: ". . . he looked upon us as a sort of animals to whose share, by what accident he could not conjecture, some small pittance of Reason had fallen, whereof we made no other use than by its assistance to aggravate our *natural* corruptions, and to acquire new ones which nature had not given us." This time Gulliver agrees: "When I thought of my family, my friends, my countrymen, or human race in general, I considered them as they really were, Yahoos in shape and disposition, perhaps a little more civilized, and qualified with the gift of speech, but making no other use of reason than to improve and multiply those vices whereof their brethren in this country had only the share that nature allotted them."

It is as a thorough misanthrope that Gulliver returns home.

When his loving wife greets him affectionately, he swoons, "having not been used to the touch of that odious animal [his wife!] for so many years." The swoon lasted a long time, "almost an hour," for Gulliver's revulsion is now compounded. His wife has a "smell" which is not only (as with the perfumed Brobdingnagian maidens) physically overpowering, but now also morally unbearable. She is a Yahoo. He never even asks about their baby, born after he left home.

Gulliver's travels end with what is generally agreed to be a searing indictment of mankind. Gulliver himself states what has happened: ". . . the many virtues of those excellent quadrupeds [the Houyhnhnms] placed in opposite view to human corruptions, had so far opened my eyes and enlarged my understanding, that I began to view the actions and passions of man in a very different light, and to think the honour of my own kind not worthy managing." Gulliver has finally assessed; and the result of that assessment is the judgment which resolves the tension of the entire book: mankind is Yahoo.

VII   *The Curtain of Gloom*

I am convinced that Swift would, in the main, have endorsed Gulliver's terrible indictment. Certainly man, though no doubt a child of God, has in him Yahoo potentialities and not uncommonly behaves in true Yahoo fashion. To applaud the doctrine is not necessarily to applaud the man, however. Gulliver is not applauded. In fact, as Book IV progresses, the voice of Swift with increasing insistence condemns Gulliver for his foolish behavior.

In the first place, *all* men in the world defined by this book are not Yahoos. Pedro de Mendez, the captain in whose ship Gulliver traveled back to Europe, is by Gulliver's own description "a very courteous and generous person." He therefore "descended to treat him *like an animal* [my italics] which had some little portion of reason." To say that Swift intended Don Pedro as a kind of test of Gulliver's judgment is obviously a thesis beyond demonstration. It suggests a more sophisticated narrative skill than most people would credit Swift with. However, Don Pedro does in fact serve as a test, whether Swift intended it or not; and it is a test which Gulliver fails. A writer could hardly more clearly indicate Gulliver's status as a reporter. Readers will recall how relatively trust-worthy Gulliver was in the acccount of his first voyage. Though we had occasionally to be on our guard (as when he missed the point of how "lenient" the Lilliputians would have been had they blinded him and then starved him to death), he was on the whole about as responsible a reporter as we could reasonably expect to find. The Gulliver who thinks Don Pedro is an "animal" has for-feited our trust.

Gulliver also errs with respect to the Houyhnhnms. Though possessing some ideal traits ("Friendship and Benevolence are the two principal virtues among the Houyhnhnms," he reports), his hosts are not ideal and are not intended to be so. Many studies have helped to settle this point. For example, Ernest Tuveson has pointed out that Swift's religious convictions, convictions which he held strongly and sincerely, would obviously prevent him from offering the Houyhnhnms to us as ideal.[35] The metaphor might also have presented problems if Swift had intended the horse as an unqualified ideal. A reader tends to identify himself with that which an author considers attractive, if he respects the au-thor. It is not likely that many adult readers, in their right mind, care to equate themselves with horses. Virtues may be con-vincingly personified; but, if any degree of sophistication is de-sired, they cannot be convincingly "horse-ified."

That the voices of Gulliver and of Swift are usually separate in Book IV—and an interpretation of what these two voices are say-ing—is impressively stated in John F. Ross's "The Final Comedy of Lemuel Gulliver." The majority of the responsible critical stud-ies in the past two decades have been influenced by Ross's con-clusion.[36] The substance of this conclusion is simply that Swift has two satiric butts in Book IV: man and Gulliver. Man always can be, and too often is, as Gulliver says in Book IV, "a lump of de-formity and diseases, both in body and mind, smitten with *pride*." In other words, man = Yahoo and is, in fact, often worse than Yahoo. On the evidence that Gulliver offers, he was as right as rain when he said that, and I believe Swift agreed with this indict-ment. But, while approving the indictment, Swift would have disapproved of the indictor's reaction to this judgment. For ex-ample, Gulliver's swooning "for almost an hour" when his wife embraces him is really an insane reaction, however reasonable it seems to Gulliver. Equally neurotic is the way he treats his family: five years after his return, they are still not allowed to touch his bread or drink out of the same cup, or even to take him by the hand. Furthermore, Gulliver all this while "trots like a horse"; he spends four hours every day talking to horses. He is obviously trying to force to reality this insane metaphor (he = horse) in a frenetic attempt to avoid that other equally insane one (he = Yahoo), and when last seen, he is an object of amused pity. As Professor Ross states, Gulliver has "gone off the deep end and cannot recover himself from the nightmare view of man." [37]

The satire of Book IV of *Gulliver's Travels* is, therefore, two-edged: it is against all men, for their meanness, their self-pollution, and their pride; against Gulliver (or anyone like him) for an absurd response to the discovery of what seems to him to be the true nature of man.

CHAPTER 7

Recapitulation and Assessment

E ACH part of Swift's first major prose work may be read singly. However, similarities in tone, point of view, and major themes make it easy and in some ways preferable to regard the three parts of this first work—*A Tale of a Tub, The Battle of the Books,* and *The Mechanical Operation of the Spirit* (1704, 1710)— as contributing to one whole. So viewed, the *Tale*-volume's dominating satiric target is irrationality. Because man allows his "fancy" to get "astride his reason" and his "imagination" to be "at cuffs with his senses," "common understanding, as well as common sense, is kicked out of doors." Since it is clear that abuses in religion and in learning are inexorably the consequence of such irrational behavior, it must be granted that Swift succeeded with his intention, as stated in the "Apology" to the 1710 edition of the *Tale:* "The abuses in Religion, he proposed to set forth in the Allegory of the Coats, and the three Brothers, which was to make up the body of the discourse. Those in learning he chose to introduce by way of digressions."

However, though the *Tale*-volume does achieve its stated purpose and though the book has its moments of tremendous brilliance, it is not so great a book as *Gulliver's Travels.* Not only is the narrative and thematic tension of the *Travels* more expertly sustained, but Gulliver is a far more convincing "narrator" than the "modern hack" who purports to be the writer of the *Tale*-volume. These factors are perhaps sufficient to account for the feeling of dissatisfaction that I and many other readers feel when we finish the *Tale*-volume as a whole, or any part of it, and when we then attempt to assess its merits.

I suggest, however, that the trouble lies also in another and more serious demonstration of Swift's lack of control over his materials: his book says more than he apparently intended it to say, and unfortunately this "more" sometimes contradicts the stated intentions of the author. Thus, for example, if he is to support the Ancients in a "battle" against the Moderns, he should not begin his account by insisting upon the triviality and animality of the whole affair. It is a crippling tactical blunder to assert on his opening page that "war is the child of pride," for the comment, if it is true at all, must obviously embrace this particular "battle"; furthermore, it is irreparably damaging to proclaim that, "to speak in the phrase of writers upon politics, we may observe in the Republic of Dogs (which, in its original, seems to be an institution of the many), . . . that civil broils arise among them when it happens for one great bone to be seized on by some leading dog. . . ." The image does not even sort out the "ancient" dogs from the "modern" dogs in the quarrel; all of them are dogs.

Again, though we must allow the fact that the *Tale* does sharply illuminate the nature of the abuses in religion and in learning, we must also allow that the satire strikes as hard at Swift's own church as it does at the churches he was presumably attacking; and, although we are willing to agree that the use of common sense would redress all abuses in religion and in learning, we are forced to note that this hopeful possibility is precluded if, among the lot of us, we cannot muster so much as a thimbleful of common sense.

Perhaps if Swift had managed to keep enough distance between himself and his narrator, he might have succeeded. But too often he allowed himself to be ensnared by his own intense involvement in the situation he was describing. The distance between him and his speaker (his tale-teller) is as a consequence so slight and so very narrow that we are inclined to hear *not* the tale-teller but Swift himself say (Section IX) that "if we take an examination of what is generally understood by happiness, as it has respect either to the understanding or the senses, we shall find all its properties and adjuncts will herd under this short definition, that it is a perpetual possession of being well deceived." Though irony may well have been intended by the remark, it is an irony that, at least for some of us, does not succeed. Again (Section VIII) we hear not "the learned Aeolist maintain . . ." but Swift himself maintaining that "the original cause of all things [is] wind, from which principle this whole universe was at first produced. . . ."

In a world so formed, there is no reason. There simply is no common sense that can sally out and be "at cuffs" with "fancy." Thus inextricably threaded into and through the fabric of the *Tale*-volume are images and ideas that, refusing to be confined by Swift's too narrow statement of intention, end up in truth by revealing its inadequacies. The confusion is unsettling to the reader and is perhaps the best reason why, while so tremendously admiring the great high points in this book, we feel at the last a dissatisfaction with it.

I *The Poetry*

A comparable dissatisfaction with Swift's poetry occurs only if we are expecting too much or are looking for qualities that his poetry simply does not possess. For example, there is no rapture and no lyric note; there is little use made of metaphor; and much of the poetry is quite trivially occasional—like an invitation to Dr. Sheridan, to come to dinner, or like any other of the scores of inconsequential poems which he himself called "family trifles." However, even in some of these poems which have little or no poetic merit there are lines which are interesting as expressions of themes that are dominant in the prose and in his thinking generally. "To Mr. Congreve" (1693), for example, compares critics to asses ("Nor need the lion's skin conceal the ass"), and this so familiar use of *"le mythe animal"* will appear in almost the same form in the "Digression concerning Critics" in *A Tale of a Tub* (1704). Also, in this same poem, Swift cuts at the pseudoscientism of "virtuosoes . . . dissecting flies," and this he does again, more than thirty years later, in Book III of *Gulliver's Travels* (1726). Moreover, in the poetry he uses satiric methods that he also employs with superb effect in the prose works. For example, one of his better poems, "A Beautiful Young Nymph" (1731), achieves much of its great power because, just as in *Gulliver's Travels*, its author distorts reality by describing it only partially and then by exaggerating the features even of those parts. The distortion results in caricature, but it is not caricature that we can laugh at or be comfortable with. Its maker's fierce indignation and passionate conviction are too apt to compel a disturbing measure of agreement.

However, of these various reasons for reading Swift's poetry, the most sensible one is that it deserves and rewards study. For, at its best, it can be wonderfully conversational and witty (as in "Verses on the Death of Dr. Swift." [1732]); it can be brilliantly and brutally satirical (as in the "Satirical Elegy On the Death of a late Famous General" [1722]); it can be teasing and tender (as in "Stella's Birth-day" [1721]); and (as in "A City Shower" [1710] or in "To Stella" [1720]) it can bring to poetry facts which the main stream of poetry has until our time tended to ignore. Everybody sees the rainbow after a city shower, if there is a rainbow; it is a rare man who, like Swift, pretty much ignores the rainbow and studies what is always there—the gutter—and notes, after the shower, "Sweepings from Butchers Stalls, Dung, Guts, and Blood,/ Drown'd Puppies, Stinking Sprats, all drench'd in Mud,/ Dead Cats and Turnip-Tops . . . tumbling down the Flood." These too are facts.

II Gulliver's Travels

Any fairly representative collection of books about Swift will reveal how persistent has been the tendency to see a pattern in his life and writings and to try to understand what this pattern means. Such a reaction is natural and normal with respect to his life, and it is also necessary if we have seriously confronted his writings. The very great danger, however, is that our epithets that describe these patterns may seem forever to settle all the problems and unravel all the puzzles. This danger, most especially present in any account of the life and writings of so complex a figure as Swift, compels belief that there is something, and sometimes quite a lot, left over after we have read *Swift, or the Egotist; Jonathan Swift, Dean and Pastor; The Conjured Spirit; Giant in Chains; Swift and the Age of Compromise;* or *The Appeal to Reason.*

Swift did, or was, or exemplified all of what these titles suggest; but puzzles still remain; and they are still fairly numerous. Among them is the question of his relationship with women, particularly with Stella and with Esther Vanhomrigh. We wonder why when he was young and living with Sir William Temple, he did not more vigorously prosecute the advancement of his own career. Why did he "renounce" poetry in 1693? Why was he not awarded a bishopric in 1713? What was the reason for delaying the publication of the *Tale*-volume? How accurately does the imagery in the *Tale*-volume, and elsewhere, reveal his deep-seated, unarticulated, but nonetheless very real conviction about man? Of the hundreds of sermons that he preached, why are we left with so few of them? Even if he was careless with his sermon manuscripts and deemed them of no great consequence, there were plenty of people around who could be presumed to treasure them and perhaps want to profit from them. Swift was very careless with his poetry manuscripts, but three volumes of poetry in Sir Harold Williams' edition testify to the interest that other people had in collecting and putting into print any and every scrap of verse that the dean ever put his hand to and that they could get a hold of. Why did they not do the same with his sermons? Why do we have only eleven or twelve of them? Again, what interpretation should we give to the "little language" in *The Journal To Stella* and in *Gulliver's Travels?* Larger questions, relevant to any great literary works, also still abide: specifically, for example, what *is* the meaning of *Gulliver's Travels,* or of *A Tale of a Tub,* or of *The Modest Proposal,* or of *The Journal to Stella?* We may essay answers to these and numerous other puzzles, but some of these puzzles will remain, continually commanding our interest.

However, the known facts of Swift's life and the many goodly towers that are his literary productions do reveal a sky line, so to say, that almost any careful reader of Swift would immediately recognize as "Swiftean." If part of this man and his writings still resists our most persistent and studious inquiry, we can yet admit the existence of what Quintana calls "a picture . . . reasonably complete and consistent." [1]

Gulliver's Travels gives us both the "reasonably complete and consistent" picture and also something of the enigmatic nature of the genius that envisioned the world which that book defines. We recall that Book I of the *Travels* shows us an archetypal average man named Lemuel Gulliver who, in relation to the various forms of pettiness and meanness in Lilliput, seems commendably humane and good-hearted. Book I also introduces several problems which we must cope with early in our reading of that book. One of these, the problem of scatology (Swift's "bathroom complex") has in the past infected and warped responses to the *Travels,* to the poems, and to much of the *Tale*-volume. It need not do so today. Another problem has to do with Swift's topical satire, for—especially in Book I and Book III—there are numerous very specific references to men and events of Swift's own day. A knowledge of the considerable data which have an immediate contemporary application does certainly enrich our reading of the *Travels,* but an awareness of such data is of secondary importance to an awareness of the satire that is timeless. Flimnap is to be sure Robert Walpole, but more importantly he is any politician who wins and maintains power solely by his adroitness in walking, or even doing tricks on, the political "tightrope." A third oft-mentioned problem is that of the "little language" in the *Travels,* a language which, though attracting considerable scholarly concern, must in our present state of knowledge be thought primarily, if not exclusively, merely an effective versimilar device: this is how residents do talk in these never-never lands. A final problem has to do with Swift's narrator (Gulliver), a narrator whose effectiveness is so great that his only competition in the Swift canon is from the projector of the "modest proposal" and, in Swift's own day, with "M.B.," the humble drapier. Gulliver is a likable, fairly responsible reporter whom we want to trust completely but never quite can and whom, at the end of the fourth voyage, we have to dismiss as incompetent.

Book I introduces major satiric themes, too, like the satire on the ingratitude of princes and on the empty pomposity of titles. The Lilliputian emperor, whose height is all of six and a half inches, has eight names to carry around: Golbasto Momaren Evlame Gurdilo Shefin *Mully Ully Gue* (my italics). The burden, especially of those last three names, is enough to crush an ordinary man; but this nobleman, who is "taller," squint-eyed Gulliver absurdly reports, "than the sons of men," seems pleased with the premise: the bigger the title, the bigger the man. Obviously, both he and his subjects needed Montaigne's healthy reminder, in "Of Experience": "So it is no use for us to mount on stilts, for on stilts we must still walk with our own legs. And in the loftiest throne in the world we are still sitting on our own behind."

Book I has other satiric targets: the travelers who, as hosts, torture guests with tiresome and almost endless recitals of everything about their trip, including their bowel movements; the trivial arguments in religion and in politics. It is as though Swift were to say, "When we argue these matters, let us not make a religious issue over which end of an egg should be broken first; or a political argument over what kind of heels to wear on our shoes: argument in these areas should be over matters of more import." Finally, Chapter 6 of Book I raises to prominence a central question which poor Gulliver will not even recognize as a question for years and a question that, once recognized, he will not attempt to answer until late in his last voyage. The question is, will this world-traveler, seeing near-utopian civilization in Book I, notice any difference between what he sees on his trip and what he sees at home? Will he compare? Will he assess? At the end of Book I, Gulliver makes no assessment. The voyage taught him nothing, so far as we can tell.

Book II continues with familiar Swiftean themes. The need for personal cleanliness is once more expressed (in chapters 1 and 4) and echoes his advise to the young friend in *The Letter to a Young Lady* (1723): wash often enough and thoroughly enough to avoid the charge of being at once "very fine and very filthy." Most important in this book, however, is the contrast between Gulliver's moral stature and the moral stature of his hosts. That they tower both physically *and morally* over Gulliver is most vividly seen in a confrontation scene when, on the basis of evidence Gulliver has furnished him, the large-souled Brobdingnagian ruler dispassionately concludes that "the bulk of your natives [are] the most pernicious race of little odious vermin that nature ever suffered to crawl upon the surface of the earth." The indictment astonishes Gulliver, who can only attribute its severity to "a certain *narrowness of thinking*, from which we and the politer countries of Europe are wholly exempted." (We note in passing how perfectly successful Swift's irony can be and very often is!) Gullible Gulliver is still the *ingénu* in this cast of characters. This voyage, like the first one, has taught him nothing.

The Gulliverian mask is used in Book III so very incidentally that we might as well forget about it: for the most part we hear Swift speaking in his own person. Satiric themes are, again, themes that we have come to recognize as part of the pattern of Swift's thought: the refusal to accept as scientific all activity that is called scientific; the satire on false and useless learning; the abuse of human talents employed in trivial ends; and the opposition to English tyranny—an opposition that Swift had expressed less allegorically but even more forcefully in 1724, with the fourth of *The Drapier Letters*, where he had said, ". . . by the Laws of God, of NATURE, of NATIONS, and of your own Country, you ARE and OUGHT to be as FREE a People as your Brethren in England."

In addition, Book III ridicules "prostitute" historians who pretend to be "truly informed of the springs and motives of great enterprises"; and it satirizes naïve ideas about immortality. As the last line of his sermon "Upon Sleeping in Church" avers, "Surely, Brethren, these Things ought not so to be." Finally, implicit in Book III, just as in so much of his other major writings, is the insistence on the paramount importance of the mind and on the imperative need to see beneath the surface of things. We are reminded that such Swiftean touchstones appear also in, for example, "Stella's Birth-day" (1721), and in *The Letter to a Young Gentleman* (1720), and often in the *Tale*-volume (1704 and 1710); but such reminders are misleading if thy suggest that the themes are anything less than pervasive in the Swift lexicon.

Book IV of *Gulliver's Travels* finds Gulliver confronting two sharply defined distortions. The first of these distortions reflected in the mirror of his mind is the picture of the Houyhnhnm-masters: to Gulliver they appear to be perfection and he accepts this appearance as the truth of the matter. The other distortion insists that Gulliver in all essentials looks like, behaves like, and in fact is, a Yahoo; this image Gulliver strenuously resists. The resistance ends and the climax comes when a female Yahoo, "inflamed by desire," attempts to violate Gulliver when he has stripped himself naked in order to bathe and wash himself in a stream. The attempt precipitates the humbling admission which relieves the major tension of the entire four books: "now I could no longer deny that I was a real Yahoo in every line and feature, since the females had a natural propensity to me, as one of their own species." If Gulliver is Yahoo—if Everyman is Yahoo—then the civilization which he and Everyman represent is also Yahoo. In the light of the Houyhnhm culture, and with the help of "lectures" from his Houyhnhnm-master and the "discources of him and his friends," Gulliver thus finally assesses the worth of his own civilization: "When I thought of my family, my friends, my countrymen, or human race in general, I considered them as they really were, Yahoos in shape and disposition, perhaps a little more civilized and qualified with the gift of speech, but making no other use of reason than to improve and multiply those vices whereof their brethren [the Yahoos] in this country [the land of the Houyhnhnms] had only the share that nature allotted them "

Full freighted with neuroses, an unhappy and misanthropic Gulliver left the land of the horses on February 15, 1714–15, at 9 o'clock in the morning." The sorrel nag ("who always loved me") whinnied (Gulliver says "cried"!) after him, "Hnuy illa nyha majah Yahoo."

III *Assessment*

Students often protest that Swift's writings lose a dimension by one striking omission: they do not explicitly give any positive and affirmative solutions to the problems posed with such startling clarity. Thus in *Gulliver's Travels* Swift shows us what our response should not be, but he does not show us what our response should be, if a clear-sighted view of the human condition perforce drives us also to a conclusion as bleak as his. Consequently, this book and all his other principal writings seem to some critics to achieve their greatest brilliance by a solely negative impact. F. R. Leavis says, "We have, then, in [Swift's] writings probably the most remarkable expression of negative feelings and attitudes that literature can offer—the spectacle of creative powers . . . exhibited consistently in negation and in rejection." [2]

The negations do imply affirmations, and these affirmations are not hard to find in *Gulliver's Travels* or, indeed, in anything Swift ever wrote. Such critics as F. R. Leavis should perhaps allow, more than they do, for this fact The affirmations are the sort that we might expect from a man whose custom it was to celebrate his birthday by reading Job 3:3: "Let the day perish wherein I was born, and the night in which it was said, 'There is a man child conceived.'" Thus, as an instance, the affirmative aspect of *Gulliver's Travels* will never incite anybody to write a battle hymn or a hymn of thanksgiving, but the affirmations are nonetheless there. Indeed, it is not difficult to see at least something of the affirmations in all of Swift's major prose and poetry—and fairly satisfactorily to explain their meaning and impact. No doubt this meaning and this impact are not exactly the same for all readers, for each good reader must inevitably respond somewhat differently to any literary work.

Inevitably and necessarily, however, a thoughtful person rising from a reading of a great writer and his works will try to find a fairly specific place in what seems to him a sane area of interpretation; he tries to make some sort of assessment of what the writings of this great figure finally amount to, today—though, even as he makes the judgment, he is aware of how hazardous and inadequate such attempts always are. In attempting to reach a sensible assessment of those writings of Swift which are most read in our times—and an assessment consistent with the positions taken in earlier pages of this book—I think we might begin by trying to understand something about Swift's distorted vision. Probably that is the place to begin with any artist, for distortion, at least in the sense of limitation of focus, is essential to art. Also, distortion is a relative matter that defines the uniqueness of each of us: it is the way each of us has of looking at things.

Swift's way of seeing things—his distortion—seems to me to be marked in the main by two attributes. The first might be called the "dead cat" syndrome, for after a rain storm he saw "Dead Cats and Turnip-Tops" in the gutter; and that is probably about the only type of thing he did see. William Carlos Williams' homely-lovely "red wheel/ barrow/ glazed with rain/ water/ beside the white chickens/" I am quite sure Swift would never have noticed and would not have thought worth notice. Looking at a Brobdingnagian female nursing a baby, Swift's little Gulliver saw what, and only what, he himself would have seen: the "monstrous breast" with a "nipple . . . about half the bigness of my head . . . and the dug so varified with spots, pimples and freckles, that nothing could appear more nauseous." This is the only detail he gives us about the appearance of this woman; and, though it is a distortion that is a caricature, it is also an incredibly honest bit of reporting. Confronted by the fact of this huge and horrid dug, who could honestly pretend to see anything else? Occasionally, in other words, Swift's distorted vision (his genius) saw exactly the single repulsive detail which so dominates a picture that it destroys any chance of, in fact eliminates any reason for, a fairer fuller, and more tolerant view.

Another attribute of Swift's vision we might term "the peeled orange" syndrome. In the works we have focused on in these pages we have seen how often it was compulsive with him to peel away the outside of things, for the outside is a fraud that cheats us of the truth. So we must stand by to see a woman "flayed" and, in our naïveté, be surprised "how much it altered her person for the worse" (Section IX of the *Tale*). If we see "the carcass of a beau" stripped, we will be "all amazed to find so many unsuspected faults under one suit of clothes" (Section IX of the *Tale*). Swift will insist that we make a prostitute remove not only her finery, but everything; for only then will we discover her "shancres [cankers], issues, [and] running sores" ("A Beautiful Young Nymph Going to Bed"). We must hound out of business a charlatan named John Partridge, whose almanacs attacked the clergy of the Church of England; but we must realize that the real reason this charlatan is more than merely a silly joke is that he pretends in his prophecies to a knowledge he does not have. So we must be made not only to see him as he is—a hypocrite—but *to care about it*.

These two attributes of Swift's vision enabled him in his best works to seize unerringly upon the single most telling detail, or pattern of details, in any situation. Usually it is only in retrospect that we recognize his technique and realize the nature of his distortions. As we read his works, however, protest is, as a rule, stalled off by his sure conviction that, as part of his community of reasonable men and women, we care about the things that he cares about: therefore he will assume that we understand and approve his dry chuckle; that we also share unreservedly and completely in his concern, his anxiety, his distress, his revulsion, or his hatred. In his greatest writings, it is the distress, the revulsion, and the hatred that are most insistently communicated; for this was a man who relived with a terrific intensity each moment that, recollecting, he chose to record. The totality of moments are salted with fun and frolic, to be sure; but the final impression is not so much negative as merely grim since the threshhold of hope in a world where "happiness . . . is a perpetual possession of being well deceived" (Section IX of the *Tale*) is predictably quite low. It is so low that Swift's addiction to the thesis that Reason is the cure-all is properly regarded as a theme sincerely expressed but its subtleties largely unexamined; in short, to a degree illusionary. Far more convincing are his pronouncements about the baleful effects of folly, or absence of reason, and the overriding need to get beneath the surface of things, for only then—this positive exhortation avers—will we see things as they really are.

But also at the heart of Swift's teaching we find the affirmation that seems to me his most viable contribution to our times: it is the affirmation that a clear and honest view of life will show how rare and how spectacular is that triumph which manages just to hold its own against the forces of dirt, of pretense, of pride, and of evil in our world. Man's odds against these forces being so nearly hopeless, his most stunningly victorious accomplishments must necessarily be simple ones: for example, as *Gulliver's Travels* puts it, to make "two blades of grass to grow upon a spot of ground where only one grew before."

For some readers the affirmation implicit in this grim vision of *Gulliver's Travels* is not relieved by a reading of Swift's other most important literary productions. It is not, I confess, for me. At the same time, however, it is at least significantly commented on by outside biographical data. We recall that Gulliver's response to his vision was neurotic: he spent at least four hours a day in talk with his horses; he trotted like a horse. Swift's response to his vision was to spend many of his best moments, for nearly half a century, as a priest of the Church of Ireland.

However, even as we note the vocation to which he so arduously and for so many years gave himself, we think of his comment in a letter to Ford (June 22, 1736): "I have long given up all hopes of Church or Christianity." [3] It seems to me that the life belies the rhetoric, for his actions strongly suggest that, in his work as dean and pastor and patriot, he never relinquished the obstinate hope that he might yet get the other blade of grass to grow. Whatever he may have thought of his contemporaries in Ireland, the majority of them were convinced that this was his intention and that he therefore gave his life "for the universal improvement of mankind." In such terms, at any rate, I find the best possible explanation of the obituary which his printer George

Faulkner wrote in *The Dublin Journal,* just after his friend's death. Of all the comments written on and for this occasion, Faulkner's tribute is my favorite; it bespeaks great admiration and affection:

Last Saturday [October 19, 1745] at three o' Clock in the Afternoon dyed that great and eminent Patriot the Rev. Dr. Jonathan Swift, Dean of St. Patrick's Dublin, in the 78th Year of his Age, . . . His Genius, Works, Learning, and Charity are so universally admired, That for a News Writer to attempt his Character would be the highest Presumption. Yet as the Printer hereof is proud to acknowledge his infinite Obligations to that Prodigy of Wit, he can only lament, that he is by no Means equal to so bold an Undertaking.

Without diminishing Swift, the modest Faulkner's warm obituary does perhaps simplify him more than the record permits. We will keep the record accurate and therefore allow that, though the outlines of the pattern are clear and consistent enough, our insights into the nature of this man and the techniques and quality of his writing are instinct still with an occasional unsolved puzzle. It is inevitably so, for truly, as Esther Vanhomrigh said in one of her letters to him, "never any one liveing thought like you." [4]

Notes and References

Chapter One

1. Herbert Davis, ed., *The Prose Works of Jonathan Swift* (Oxford, II), x.
2. *Ibid.*, 145.
3. *Ibid.*, 155.
4. *Ibid.*, 161.
5. Ricardo Quintana, *The Mind and Art of Jonathan Swift* (New York, 1936), p. 364.
6. New York, 1895, pp. 142–43.
7. New York, 1955, p. 92.
8. *Ibid.*, p. 101.
9. Irvin Ehrenpreis, *Swift: the Man, his Works, and the Age* (London, 1962), I, 69.
10. *Ibid.*, 62.
11. *Ibid.*
12. Davis, *Works*, V, 192.
13. The evidence has been assembled by Maxwell B. Gold in *Swift's Marriage to Stella* (Cambridge [Massachusetts], 1937). See also my comments in Chapter III, below.
14. Harold Williams, ed., *The Journal to Stella* (Oxford, 1948), I, p. xxix.
15. Davis, *Works*, V, 193.
16. *The Personality of Swift* (London, 1958), p. 119.
17. Davis, *Works*, V, 193.
18. "During the eighteenth century clerical preferment was a thing of the market-place" (Louis Landa, *Swift and the Church of Ireland* [Oxford, 1954], 193).
19. F. Elrington Ball, *The Correspondence of Jonathan Swift* (London, 1910–1914), IV, 137 ("Swift to Bolingbroke," March 21, 1730).
20. *Journal to Stella*, II, 662.
21. "I seldom walk less than four miles, sometimes six, eight, ten or more, never beyond my limits,; or, if it rains, I walk as much

through the house, up and down stairs. . . ." Ball, *Corresp.*, VI, 92–93 ("Swift to John Barber," August 8, 1738).

22. Louis Landa, ed., *Irish Tracts* (1720–1723) *and Sermons* (Oxford, 1948), p. ix.

23. King George I had granted to William Wood the right to send great quantities of copper halfpence to Ireland. Wood's profit from this venture would of course have been tremendous. Swift believed that the coins would so drain gold and silver from Ireland that the country would be left with a debased and inflated currency. In *The Drapier Letters* he successfully contributed to the organization of Irish resistance against the importation of the new copper coin. (See Chapter 4, above, for additional details.)

24. Davis, *Works*, V, 79. (Davis does not date this piece. Presumably it was written before 1714, however, when Swift left England.)

25. Cited in John Traugott's *Discussions of Jonathan Swift* (Boston, 1963), p. 83, from George Orwell's *Shooting an Elephant and Other Essays*.

26. *Swift, An Introduction* (New York, 1955), p. 124.

27. Cited by Quintana, *Introduction*, p. 3.

28. Ehrenpreis, *The Personality of Jonathan Swift*, p. 125.

29. Louis Landa, *Swift and the Church of Ireland* (Oxford, 1954), pp. 192–93.

30. John Hawkesworth, *The Works of Jonathan Swift* (London, 1755), I, 45. For the use of this splendid edition I owe thanks to Dr. Howard Burton.

31. Ball, *Corresp.*, V, 415 ("Swift to Pope," February 9, 1737).

32. Ehrenpreis, *The Personality of Swift*, p. 123.

33. *Ibid.*, 123.

34. Hawkesworth, *Works*, I, 58.

35. "Verses on the Death of Dr. Swift" (1731), line 482.

36. *Collected Essays in Literary Criticism* (London, 1938), p. 196.

37. *Ibid.*

Chapter Two

1. Ehrenpreis, *Swift*, I, 226–28.

2. Translated from *Swift, les années de jeunesse et le "Conte du Tonneau"* (Strasbourg and London, 1925), p. 256. Here and throughout this study, translations from Pons's great book are my own.

3. Ehrenpreis, *Swift*, I, 62.

4. A. C. Guthkelch and D. Nichol Smith, eds., *A Tale of a Tub* (Oxford, 1958), p. 206, fn. 1. On the subject of the dating of the *Tale*, see also Ehrenpreis, *Swift*, I, 186–87.

5. See Ehrenpreis, *Swift*, I, 186, for a recent discussion of this problem. See also Pons, *op. cit.*, Section II, Chapter 1.

6. See Guthkelch and Smith, eds., *A Tale of a Tub*, p. xlviii, for speculation about this problem.

7. Quintana, *The Mind and Art of Swift*, pp. 86–96.

8. Pp. 244–46.

9. E.g., (a) "[I]f I had not been a good swimmer, it might have gone very hard with me" (Bk. II, Ch. 3); (b) "I could not swim a league" (Bk. IV, Ch. 10); (a) "I would never be an instrument of bringing a free and brave people into slavery" (Bk. I, Ch. 5); (b) Gulliver criticizes the Brobdingnagian king for his willingness to "let slip an opportunity put into his hands that would have made him absolute master of the lives, liberties, and the fortunes of his people" (Bk. II, Ch. 7); (a) Gulliver protests "so inviolable an attachment to truth" (Bk. II, Ch. 7); (b) Shortly after, "pretending I was sick, [I] kept close to my cabin" (Bk. IV, Ch. 11); etc. Inconsistencies in the *Tale*-volume will be mentioned below: in this chapter, Part III, for example.

10. "See *Works of Swift*, 1824, vol. i, p. 89. Scott got the story from Theophilus Swift": fn. 2, p. xix, in Guthkelch and Smith, eds., *A Tale of a Tub*.

11. Davis, *Works*, I, p. xxx: "Swift suggested to his printer Benjamin Tooke that a Key should be . . . made up of quotations from Wotton's *Observations*, and Tooke improved upon this by arranging Wotton's comments as footnotes to the passages referred to, and inserting them among the other footnotes, almost certainly provided by Swift himself for this [1710] edition."

12. Cited by Quintana, *The Mind and Art of Swift*, p. 77.

13. Pons, p. 284.

14. P. 281.

15. Of course the St. James's was chosen deliberately, for Richard Bentley was Library-keeper there.

16. Émile Pons, referring to Temple's skill as a bee-keeper, suggests that it was "perhaps the greatest skill he had"! (Pons, *op. cit.*, p. 270).

17. For example: "[Swift] paid a lifetime allowance to a needy sister; he supported and regularly visited a widowed and distant mother. In his era of intimacy with peers and statesmen, he saw and gave help to humble relations. When, ageing and ill, he lived withdrawn from the world, he lent a fortune to a young cousin. . . ." Ehrenpreis, *Swift*, I, 3.

18. Quintana, *The Mind and Art of Swift*, 86–96.

19. Ehrenpreis, *Swift*, I, 188. But see Pons's comment, too. Pons

believes that in Section IV of the *Tale,* Peter becomes "a person with flesh and blood" (*op. cit.,* p. 376).

20. See C. M. Webster, "Swift's *Tale of a Tub* compared with Earlier Satires of the Puritans," *Publications of the Modern Language Association,* XLVII (1933); and "Swift and Some Earlier Satirists of Puritan Enthusiasm," *Publications of the Modern Language Association,* XLVIII (1933).

21. *The Mind and Art of Swift,* p. 96.

22. *Swift's Rhetorical Art* (New Haven, 1953), p. 91.

23. *Theme and Structure in Swift's Tale of a Tub* (New Haven, 1960), p. 234.

24. Ehrenpreis, *Swift,* I, 189.

25. "The History of Martin," which is often inserted at the end of the *Tale,* is not Swift's.

26. One interesting page in *The Mechanical Operation of the Spirit* introduces a detail which appears in modern literary history in the depiction of the preacher (Casey) of Steinbeck's *Grapes of Wrath.* Like Casey, "it has been frequent" with these dissenters "in the height and orgasmus of their spiritual exercise" to have a sexual orgasm also.

27. Boston, 1965, p. 174.

28. Cited by Landa, *Swift and the Church of Ireland,* p. xiv. Also, St. Patrick's had at this time only the base of a steeple.

29. Pons, *op. cit.,* p. 395.

30. *Ibid.,* p. 393.

Chapter Three

1. Quintana, *The Mind and Art of Swift,* p. 187. See also Davis, *Works,* VI, p. ix.

2. Richard Bentley, *A Dissertation upon the Epistles of Phalaris* (London, 1817), pp. 283–84.

3. Davis, *Works,* IV, p. xvi.

4. *Journal to Stella, op. cit.,* I, 7, and footnote.

5. *Ibid.,* p. xliv and pages following, for a discussion of this point.

6. All *Journal* quotations are from the invaluable Williams edition, cited above.

7. The *Journal's* first editors inserted the word *Stella* here, in place of some more cryptic allusion to her. Swift "at the time he wrote these letters, had not begun to call Esther Johnson by the name of Stella." (*The Journal to Stella, op. cit.,* I, p. xxiv).

8. *The Providence of Wit in the English Letter Writers* (Durham, 1955), pp. 202–3.

9. *Journal to Stella,* p. xxxvi.

10. *Works,* I, 49.

11. See e.g., Denis Johnston, *In Search of Swift* (Dublin, 1959).

Chapter Four

1. Joseph Horrell, *Collected Poems of Jonathan Swift* (London, 1958), I, p. xl: "A significant part of Swift's canon consists of (i) poems he published singly but did not collect, apparently desiring their suppression, and (ii) poems left in manuscript, often unfinished or imperfect: both classes found their way into his works after his death and even before."

2. All quotations from poems are taken from the edition by Harold Williams: *The Poems of Jonathan Swift* (Oxford, 1937).

3. Ehrenpreis, *Swift,* I, 120–30; and Émile Pons, *Swift, les années de jeunesse et le "Conte du Tonneau,"* p. 177. Also see Williams, *Poems,* I, p. xv: "[Swift] was constantly turning verses as a common part of his everyday life, so much so that no part of his writing is as complete as autobiography, . . ."

4. Maurice Johnson, *The Sin of Wit* (Syracuse [New York], 1950), pp. 6–7. See, also, Ehrenpreis, *Swift,* I, 113.

5. Quintana, *The Mind and Art of Swift,* p. 29. Herbert Davis refers to these early poems as "not by any means as uninteresting or as weak as is often suggested (*Jonathan Swift, Essays on his Satire* [New York, 1964], p. 172).

6. Ball, *Corresp.* I, 361 ("Swift to Thomas Swift," May 3, 1692).

7. *Ibid.,* 364.

8. *Ibid.,* 365.

9. Maurice Johnson, "A literary chestnut: Dryden's 'Cousin Swift'," *Publications of the Modern Language Association* LXVII (1952), 1024–34.

10. Ehrenpreis, *Swift,* I, 110. Also, in "Swift to Thomas Swift," cited above: Jonathan Swift, commenting on the "Athenian Ode" stanzas, mentioned Sir William Temple's "speaking to me so much in their praise. . . ." Praise from the great Temple meant much to Swift and apparently was sufficient inducement for him to continue work, at least for a time, in a genre that so little suited his genius.

11. Davis, *Swift, Essays on his Satire,* 171–72.

12. Quintana, *Introduction,* pp. 49–50.

13. Horrell, I, pp. xxx–xxxi.

14. *Eighteenth-Century Poetry* (New Jersey, 1964), pp. xxxiii–xxxiv.

15. Wordsworth, standing on Westminster Bridge and looking at London, said, "Earth has not anything to show more fair/ . . . This city now doth like a garment wear/ The beauty of the morning." I

doubt that Swift would have reacted in this way. More seriously, I think a limitation in his vision would not have permitted him to allow that Wordsworth's reading of this experience is not merely different from what his would have been, but is equally valid. Similarly, Donne's "To His Mistris Going to Bed" may be taken as not an equally valid, but really a far more valid depiction than Swift's "A Beautiful Young Nymph Going to Bed" (discussed below). Donne's scene in which the female disrobes would probably seem less a distortion to the average adult male, for it is closer in spirit and in tone to the lovely line in Ezekiel 37:6, where God, having made man, "clothed" him "in skin."

16. Quintana, *The Mind and Art of Swift*, p. 278.

17. Scott, *The Works of Jonathan Swift*, I ("A Life of the Author"), 272.

18. Quintana, *The Mind and Art of Swift*, p. 221.

19. George Birbeck Hill, ed., *Johnson's Lives of the English Poets* (Oxford, 1905), III, 31–32.

20. Quintana, *Introduction*, p. 19.

21. Hill, *Johnson's Lives*, III, 32.

22. Williams, *Poems*, II, 684.

23. Quintana, *The Mind and Art of Swift*, p. 238.

24. Harold Williams, *The Correspondence of Jonathan Swift* (Oxford, 1963), II, 363–64.

25. Williams, *Corresp.*, III, 130.

26. Horrell, I, p. xxxi.

27. Cited by Horrell, I, pp. lvi–lvii.

28. Cited by Horrell, I, p. lix.

29. Williams, *Poems*, I, 296.

30. Johnson, *The Sin of Wit*, p. 110. For example, commenting on Swift's writing during the years 1729–33, Jacques Pons refers to "*nombreux poèmes, dont plusieurs sont obscènes et dédiés à la gloire de la matière fécale.*" ("Notes" to *Voyages de Gulliver*, Paris: 1964 ["*le livre de poche*"], p. 442.)

31. Johnson, *The Sin of Wit*, p. 116.

32. I owe the suggestion to Constance Coulter Hunting.

33. Johnson, *The Sin of Wit*, p. 35.

34. Lewis Leary, *Whittier* (New York, 1961), p. 169.

35. *Ibid.*, p. 80.

36. Ball, *Corresp.*, IV, 328 ("Swift to Charles Wogan," August 2, 1732).

37. Hill, *Johnson's Lives*, III, 65.

38. Cited by Stanley Edgar Hyman, *The Armed Vision* (New York, 1955), p. 65.

39. From "Verses on the Death of Dr. Swift" (1732).

Chapter Five

1. Ball, *Corresp.*, IV, 137 ("Swift to Bolingbroke," March 21, 1730).
2. *Ibid.*, IV, 76 ("Swift to Bolingbroke and Pope," April 5, 1729).
3. *Ibid.*, IV, 316 (July 10, 1732).
4. Davis, *Works*, IX, 25–26.
5. *Ibid.*, p. xxii.
6. Hawkesworth, *Works*, I, 15.
7. *Swift and the Church of Ireland*, pp. 191–92.
8. *Ibid.*, 187.
9. Landa, *Irish Tracts and Sermons*, p. 98.
10. Ball, *Corresp.*, I, 29 (January 13, 1699).
11. Davis, *Works*, IX, 97 (Introduction by Louis Landa).
12. Pilkington, *Memoirs* (London, 1928), p. 50.
13. Davis, *Works*, IX, p. xxvii.
14. It might be said that Swift was trying to help his young friend in a situation which he describes in Book IV of *Gulliver's Travels:* ". . . if a female stranger came among them, three or four of her own sex would get about her, and stare and chatter and grin and smell her all over and then turn off with gestures that seemed to express contempt and disdain."
15. Cited by Hawkesworth, *Works*, I, 70.
16. Davis, *Works*, IX, p. xxvii.
17. Cited by Katherine Hornbeak in her article on the identity of "the very young lady," in the *Huntington Library Quarterly*, VII (February, 1944), 184, from Mrs. Pilkington's *Memoirs*.
18. *The Prose Works of Swift* (London, 1907), XI, 115.
19. Émile Pons, *op. cit.*, p. 327 and *passim*.
20. Cited by Davis, *Works*, XII, pp. xix–xx.
21. *Swift's Rhetorical Art*, p. 71.
22. David Nichol Smith, *Letters to Ford* (Oxford, 1935), 85–86.
23. Quintana, *Introduction*, p. 124. See also Oliver W. Ferguson, *Jonathan Swift and Ireland* (Urbana, 1962), pp. 136, 186.
24. This quotation and those that follow (all from the *Short View*) are from Davis, *Works*, XII, 8–11.
25. Quintana, *Introduction*, 167.
26. Davis, *Works*, X, 63.
27. Edward Rosenheim, *Swift and the Satirist's Art* (Chicago, 1963), pp. 47–51.

Chapter Six

1. Pope's words, cited by Quintana, *The Mind and Art of Swift*, p. 206.

2. *Ibid.*, 207.

3. Quintana, *Introduction*, p. 144; and for a more extended discussion, see William Eddy, *"Gulliver's Travels": A Critical Study* (Princeton, 1923).

4. Quintana, *Introduction*, p. 105.

5. See the useful summary of relevant information in D. Nichol Smith, *The Letters of Swift to Ford* (Oxford, 1935), pp. xxxix–xl.

6. Ball, *Corresp.*, V, 180 ("Swift to Pulteney," May 12, 1735).

7. Ball, *Corresp.*, III, 276 (September 29, 1725).

8. Smith, *Letters of Swift to Ford*, p. 158.

9. Ball, *Corresp.*, III, 356 (November 5, 1726).

10. *Ibid.*, III, 358–59 (November 17, 1726).

11. But see Quintana, *The Mind and Art of Swift*, pp. 303–6; and see "The Criticism of Gulliver's 'Voyage to the Houyhnhnms,'" 1726–1914," by Merrel D. Clubb, in *Stanford Studies in Language and Literature* (Stanford, 1941), 203–32.

12. Hill, *Johnson's Lives*, III, 38.

13. Cited by Traugott's *Discussions of Jonathan Swift*, p. 19.

14. Leslie Stephen, *Swift* (London, 1882), p. 180.

15. Ball, *Corresp.* III, 439 ("Swift to Motte," December 28, 1727).

16. *Ibid.*

17. Edward A. Block, "Gulliver: Middle-Class Englishman," *Modern Language Notes* (November, 1953), 474–77.

18. Cited by Louis Landa, in the Norton Critical Edition of *Gulliver's Travels* (Robert Greenberg, ed., New York, 1961), p. 275. For further discussion of this matter, see also Phyllis Greenacre's *Swift and Carroll, A Psychoanalytic Study of Two Lives*, referred to in Chapter 1, above.

19. Ehrenpreis, *The Personality of Swift*, p. 49. By way of contrast, consult Jacques Pons' extraordinary "Notes" to *Voyages de Gulliver*, *op. cit.*, p. 51: *"Le goût qu'il avait de parler de la matière fécale dans se écrits incommodait fort ses contemporains. Mais loin de se corriger, il ne fera que s'enfoncer dans cette direction et consacrera des poèms entiers à la gloire des excréments."*

20. Ball, *Corresp.*, IV, 329 ("Swift to Wogan," August 2, 1732). The morality, generally there, is sometimes overwhelmed by other considerations: by satire of a literary tradition, for example ("A Description of A City Shower"); by a mixture of spleen and party spirit (the "Satirical Elegy On the Death of a late Famous General").

21. All quotations from *Gulliver's Travels* are from the Rinehart edition, edited by John F. Ross (New York, 1948).

22. This was Lewis' comment about Wells, cited by Martin Light

in "H. G. Wells and Sinclair Lewis," *English Fiction in Transition* (November, 1962), p. 5.

23. See Arthur Case's edition of *Gulliver's Travels* (New York, 1938), p. 344.

24. See George Sherburn's edition of *Gulliver's Travels* (New York, 1950), p. ix.

25. Hill, *Johnson's Lives*, III, 38.

26. For a contrary view, see, e.g., John N. Sutherland, "A Reconsideration of Gulliver's Third Voyage," *Studies in Philology*, LIV (January, 1957), 45–52.

27. "The Shadowy World of the Third Voyage" (from *Jonathan Swift and the Age of Compromise*), reprinted in the Norton Critical Edition of *Gulliver's Travels* (Robert Greenberg, ed.), p. 335.

28. See e.g., M. Nicholson and N. Mohler, "The Scientific Background of Swift's *Voyage to Laputa*," *Annals of Science*, II (July, 1937); by the same authors, "Swift's 'Flying Island' in the *Voyage to Laputa*," *Annals of Science*, II (October, 1937); George R. Potter, "Swift and National Science," *Philological Quarterly*, XX (April, 1941); Kathleen Williams, *Jonathan Swift and the Age of Compromise* (Kansas, 1958), pp. 173, and following.

29. See especially the work of Marjorie Nicholson and Nora Mohler, mentioned above.

30. See note 1, above, in this chapter.

31. Bonamy Dobrée, "Swift and Science, and the Placing of Book III," in the Norton Critical Edition of *Gulliver's Travels*, p. 330.

32. Dobrée, p. 331.

33. See his edition of *Gulliver's Travels*, referred to above, p. 344.

34. Hugo Reichard, "Gulliver the Pretender," *Papers on English Language and Literature*, I (Autumn, 1965), 321, 325.

35. "Swift: the Dean as Satirist," *University of Toronto Quarterly*, XXII (July, 1953), 368–75. Also see, among many others, Kathleen Williams, "Gulliver's Voyage to the Houyhnhnms," *Journal of English Literary History*, XVIII (December, 1951), 275–86.

36. "Studies in the Comic," *University of California Publications in English*, 1941, VIII, No. 2, pp. 175–96. See also Edward Stone, "Swift and the Horses: Misanthropy or Comedy?" *Modern Language Quarterly*, X (September, 1949), 367–76. The Ross thesis, widely accepted, is not universally accepted. For example, see the *Johnsonian News Letter* (March, 1964), p. 3, for a convenient short summary of what is there called "The sharp split between the two divisions of Swift interpreters—what we like to call the 'soft school' and the 'hard school' . . . ."

37. Ross, p. 194.

Chapter Seven

1. Quintana, *Introduction*, p. 27.
2. Cited from F. R. Leavis, *Determinations* (London, 1934), by John Traugott, ed., in his *Discussions of Swift*, p. 42.
3. Ball, *Corresp.*, V, 351.
4. Williams, *Corresp.*, II, 364.

Selected Bibliography

PRIMARY SOURCES

The Shakespeare Head edition is the best collected edition of Swift's writings. Edited by Herbert Davis and entitled *The Prose Works of Jonathan Swift* (Oxford: Oxford University Press, 1935–55), it includes thirteen volumes:

Vol. I: *A Tale of a Tub, with Other Early Works, 1696–1707.* 1939;

II: *Bickerstaff Papers and Pamphlets on the Church.* 1939;

III: *The Examiner and Other Pieces Written in 1710–11.* 1940;

IV: *A Proposal for Correcting the ENGLISH TONGUE, Polite Conversation, Etc.* 1957;

V: *Miscellaneous And Autobiographical Pieces; Fragments And Marginalia.* 1962;

VI: *Political Tracts, 1711–13.* 1951;

VII: *History of the Four Last Years of the Queen* (Introduction by Sir Harold Williams). 1951;

VIII: *Political Tracts, 1713–19.* 1953;

IX: *Irish Tracts (1720–1723) and Sermons* (ed. by Louis Landa). 1948;

X: *The Drapier's Letters and Other Works, 1724–25.* 1941;

XI: *Gulliver's Travels* (Introduction by Sir Harold Williams). 1941.

XII: *Irish Tracts, 1728–33.* 1955;

XIII: *Directions to Servants* and *Miscellaneous Pieces, 1733–1742.* 1959;

XIV: [Forthcoming: an index to the whole series].

An outstanding edition of *A Tale of a Tub, The Battle of the Books,* and *The Mechanical Operation of the Spirit* is that of A. C. Guthkelch and D. Nichol Smith (Oxford: Oxford University Press, 1920). For the poetry of Swift, there are a popular collection by Joseph Horrell, *Collected Poems of Jonathan Swift* (London: Routledge and Paul, 1958),

2 vols., and the great standard collection by Harold Williams, *The Poems of Jonathan Swift* (Oxford: Oxford University Press, 1937; revised, 1958), 3 vols. Sir Harold Williams' formidable labors have also produced the best edition of *The Journal to Stella* (Oxford University Press, 1948), 2 vols., and *The Correspondence of Jonathan Swift* (Oxford: The Clarendon Press, 1963–65), 5 vols. Because the Williams edition of the *Correspondence* was not available to me when I was writing the first draft of this book, I relied extensively on F. Elrington Ball, *The Correspondence of Jonathan Swift* (London: G. Bell and Sons, 1910–14), 6 vols., supplemented by D. Nichol Smith, *The Letters of Jonathan Swift to Charles Ford* (Oxford: The Clarendon Press, 1935). However, all quotations from the Ball edition I have since checked and corrected against the Williams edition.

SECONDARY SOURCES

1. BIOGRAPHICAL

A. *Books*

CRAIK, HENRY. *The Life of Swift*. 2 vols. London: Murray, 1894. Still the best full-length biography of Swift.

DELANEY, PATRICK. *Observations upon Lord Orrery's Remarks*. London: 1754. The best of the books by a person who knew Swift.

EHRENPREIS, IRVIN. *Mr. Swift and his Contemporaries*. London: Methuen & Co., 1962 (vol. I in a projected series of three volumes called *Swift: the Man, his Works, and the Age*).

———. *The Personality of Swift*. London: Methuen & Co., 1958. The biographical chapters in these two books by Professor Ehrenpreis are of great significance. They are superb examples of scholarly investigation.

GOLD, MAXWELL B. *Swift's Marriage to Stella, together with unprinted and misprinted letters*. Cambridge: Harvard University Press, 1937. Though harnessed to a thesis (Swift married Stella), this book is valuable for its systematic presentation of available evidence.

ISAACS, J., ed. *Memoirs of Mrs. Laetitia Pilkington*, 1712–1750. Introduction by Iris Bary. London: Routledge, 1928. Lively if not always reliable recollections of a person who knew Swift. Monck-Berkeley called her "a lying gossip."

QUINTANA, RICARDO. *Introduction*. London: Oxford University Press, 1955. Chapter One ("Swift's Career") is a valuable short account of Swift's life.

B. *Periodical Literature*

JOHNSON, MAURICE. "A literary chestnut: Dryden's 'Cousin Swift',"

Selected Bibliography

Publications of the Modern Language Association, LXVI (1952), 1024–34.

WILSON, T. G. "Swift's Deafness; and his last Illness," *Irish Journal of Medical Science*, 6th series no. 162 (June, 1939), 241–56. Reprinted in *Annals of Medical History*, 3rd series, 2 (July, 1940), 291–305.

2. GENERAL CRITICISM
A. *Books*

BULLITT, JOHN M. *Jonathan Swift and the Anatomy of Satire*. Cambridge: Harvard University Press, 1953. An attempt to define three types of satiric technique that Swift used.

EHRENPREIS, IRVIN. *The Personality of Swift*. London: Methuen and Co., 1958.

————. *Mr. Swift and his Contemporaries*. London: Methuen and Co., 1962. Impressive investigative procedures yield new insights into the personality and the biographical data of Swift's life.

EWALD, WILLIAM BRAGG, JR. *The Masks of Jonathan Swift*. Cambridge: Harvard University Press, 1954. The outstanding book so far published on Swift's use of personae.

PRICE, MARTIN. *Swift's Rhetorical Art*. New Haven: Yale University Press, 1953. An analysis of Swift's satiric technique.

QUINTANA, RICARDO. *The Mind and Art of Jonathan Swift*. London: Oxford University Press, 1936 (reprinted with additional bibliographical material, 1953). This book and the *Introduction* constitute an excellent introduction to Swift, by an eminent Swift scholar.

————. *Introduction*. London: Oxford University Press, 1955.

WATKINS, W. B. C. *Perilous Balance: the Tragic Genius of Swift, Johnson, and Sterne*. Princeton: Princeton University Press, 1939. See especially Chapter One (on Swift) and Chapter Two (on Swift and Johnson).

WILLIAMS, KATHLEEN. *Swift and the Age of Compromise*. Lawrence, Kansas: University of Kansas Press, 1958. An excellent study of Swift's understanding and use of the concept of Reason.

B. *Periodical Literature*

BROWN, JAMES. 'Swift as Moralist," *Philological Quarterly*, XXXIII (1954), 368–87.

LANDA, LOUIS A. "Swift's Economic Views of Mercantilism," *Journal of English Literary History*, X (December, 1943), 310–33.

QUINTANA, RICARDO. "Recent Discussions of Swift," *College English*, II (1940), 11–18.

SHERBURN, GEORGE. "Methods in Books about Swift," *Studies in Philology,* XXXV (October, 1938), 635–56.

3. CRITICISM OF *A Tale of a Tub*

GUTHKELCH, A. C., AND D. N. SMITH. *A Tale of a Tub To which is added The Battle of the Books and the Mechanical Operation of the Spirit.* Oxford: The Clarendon Press, 1920. A useful and justly famous edition, with very helpful introduction and notes.

HARTH, PHILIP. *Swift and Anglican Rationalism: The Religious Background of "A Tale of a Tub."* Chicago: University Press, 1961. A careful and judicious investigation.

PAULSON, RONALD. *Theme and Structure in Swift's Tale of a Tub.* New Haven: Yale University Press, 1960. An important recent examination.

PONS, ÉMILE. *Swift; les années de jeunesse et le "Conte du Tonneau."* Strasbourg: Publications de la faculté des lettres de Strasbourg, 1925. One of the classics of Swift criticism, this germinal study is particularly good on *A Tale of a Tub.*

STARKMAN, MIRIAM. *Swift's Satire on Learning in "A Tale of a Tub."* Princeton: Princeton University Press, 1950. A scholarly analysis of the satire in *A Tale of a Tub.*

4. CRITICISM OF *The Battle of the Books*

GUTHKELCH, A. C., ed. *The Battle of the Books; with Selections from the Literature of the Phalaris Controversy.* London: Chatto, 1908. Still an essential text for anyone studying this subject.

JONES, RICHARD FOSTER. *Ancients and Moderns, a Study of the Background of the Battle of the Books.* St. Louis: Washington University Studies, Language and Literature, 1936. The definitive study of the quarrel between the Ancients and the Moderns.

5. THE POETRY OF SWIFT
A. *Books*

JOHNSON, MAURICE. *The Sin of Wit: Jonathan Swift as a Poet.* Syracuse, N. Y.: Syracuse University Press, 1950. A good book-length study of Swift's poetry.

(See also, the collected editions of Swift's poems, mentioned above, edited by Joseph Horrell [*Collected Poems of Jonathan Swift*] and Harold Williams [*The Poems of Jonathan Swift*].)

B. *Periodical Literature*

DAVIS, HERBERT. "The Poetry of Jonathan Swift," *College English,* II (November, 1940), 102–15. Probably the most important fact about this appreciative article by the great Swift scholar and editor is that it reminded so many people that Swift wrote poetry, too.

6. CRITICISM OF *Gulliver's Travels*
A. *Books or Monographs*

CLUBB, MERREL D. "The Criticism of Gulliver's 'Voyage to the Houyhnhnms,' 1726–1914," in *Stanford Studies in Language and Literature,* ed. by Hardin Craig, Stanford: Stanford University Press, 1941. A fascinating report of the changing critical response to Book IV of *Gulliver's Travels.*

EDDY, WILLIAM A. *Gulliver's Travels, A Critical Study.* Princeton: Princeton University Press, 1923. The first great book-length study of the sources of *Gulliver's Travels,* it must be supplemented today by more modern investigations.

ROSS, JOHN F. "The final Comedy of Lemuel Gulliver," in *Studies in the Comic (University of California Publications in English,* vol. 8, no. 2), Berkeley, 1941. Creative criticism that helped pioneer a breakthrough in criticism of Book IV of *Gulliver's Travels.*

(See also chapters in books, cited above in this bibliography, by Bragg, Ehrenpreis, Ewald, Price, and Quintana.)

B. *Periodical Literature*

ELLIOTT, ROBERT C. "Gulliver as literary Artist," *Journal of English Literary History,* XIX (1952), 49–63.

MONK, SAMUEL H. "The Pride of Lemuel Gulliver," *Sewanee Review,* LXII (1955), 48–71.

STONE, E. "Swift and the Horses: Misanthropy or Comedy?" *Modern Language Quarterly,* X (1949), 367–76. Like Ross, Edward Stone sees the comedy in Book IV of *Gulliver's Travels.*

TUVESON, ERNEST. "Swift: the Dean as Satirist," *University of Toronto Quarterly,* XXII (1953), 368–75.

7. USEFUL RECENT PAPERBACKS

DAVIS, HERBERT. *Jonathan Swift: Essays on his Satire and Other Studies.* New York: Oxford University Press, 1964.

GREENBERG, ROBERT A., ed. *Gulliver's Travels: An Annotated Text with Critical Essays.* New York: W. W. Norton (Norton Critical Edition), 1961.

TRAUGOTT, JOHN, ed. *Discussions of Jonathan Swift.* Boston: D. C. Heath, 1962.

TUVESON, ERNEST. *Swift, A Collection of Critical Essays.* New Jersey: Prentice Hall, 1964.

8. A FINAL NOTE ON THE BIBLIOGRAPHY

The bibliography listed above is intended to be and is minimal. Something of the unusual richness of Swift criticism and scholarship will be learned if readers will note titles of numerous other distinguished articles and books not in this bibliography but mentioned in the Notes and References appended to each chapter in this book.

Also available are H. Teerink, *A Bibliography of the Writings in Prose and Verse of Jonathan Swift, D. D.* (The Hague, 1937; recently revised and corrected by Arthur H. Scouten [Philadelphia: University of Pennsylvania Press, 1963]) and Louis A. Landa and James E. Tobin, *Jonathan Swift: A List of Critical Studies Published from 1895 to 1945* (New York: Cosmopolitan Science and Art Service Co., 1945). These two essential bibliographical aids should be supplemented by "English Literature, 1660-1800: A Current Bibliography," which appears every July in the *Philological Quarterly*.

Index

Index